FARMERS VERSUS FOODIES

FARMERS VERSUS FOODIES

A Look at the Outside Forces Forging the Future of Farming and Food

RAY A. STARLING

SHORT ROWS LEADERSHIP
RALEIGH, NC

Published by
Short Rows Leadership, LLC | Raleigh, NC

Publisher's Cataloging-in-Publication Data
Starling, Ray A.

Farmers versus foodies : a look at the outside forces forging the future of farming and food / Ray A. Starling. – Raleigh, NC : Short Rows Leadership, LLC, 2022.

p. ; cm.

ISBN13: 978-0-9601147-0-2

1. Agriculture–United States. 2. Farm produce–United States. 3. Food supply–United States. I. Title.

S441.S73 2022
630.973–dc23

Project coordination by Jenkins Group, Inc. | www.jenkinsgroupinc.com

Cover design by John Barnett

Printed in the United States of America
26 25 24 23 22 • 5 4 3 2 1

Dedication

To Tina and Victoria,
who let me occupy one end of our kitchen table
with this project for the past two years.
And to the farmers and agribusiness leaders who
ensure we always have food to put on the other end.

Contents

Acknowledgments

Tina, Victoria, M.F., JoAnne, Willi, Steve, Sonny, T2, Commissioner, Mark, Andrew, Gary, Ken, Brett, Gregg, Andy, Charlie, Melissa, Chris, Chris, Angie, Sarah, Shelley, Paul, Paul, Shawn, Peter, Bill, Jarrod, Bryan, Sharon, Amber, Jake, Jordan, Steve, Nelson, Adam, Julie Anna, Chuck, Dale, Michael, Joel, Zippy, Rich, Marshall, Jay, Vernon, Kristi, Sara, Ashley, Randy, Sherry, Lucinda, Kate, Beth, Amy, Kelly, Skipper, Maggie, Tom, Randy, Michael, Ted, Barry, Julie, Kelly, Tim, MacKenna, Alex, Molly, Jeremy, Ashley, Glenn, Barry, the team at Jenkins Group, the man on the middle cross who said I could come, and countless others.

CHAPTER ONE

A REALLY BAD MEETING

It was a horrible meeting.

The new CEO of one of the most influential trade associations in Washington had just completed a face-to-face meeting with United States Secretary of Agriculture Sonny Perdue, and to say it did not go well would be like calling Union General George McClellan's 1864 presidential challenge to Abraham Lincoln a close second-place finish. Lincoln got 91 percent of the vote.

Standing on the "front porch"[1] of the second floor of the U.S. Department of Agriculture headquarters—the C-suite of a federal

1. For years prior to the Trump Administration, this area in the Department had been referred to as "the Cage." This nomenclature was not entirely unreasonable, as the doors and windows all had gridded glass panes that arguably resembled a cage. Secretary Perdue found the name to be quite unappealing, so he ordered several Cracker Barrel rocking chairs, set out some Georgia peanuts, and renamed the space the "Front Porch." Unfortunately, we never installed screen doors or trained a hound dog to sprawl out on the floor and bark when visitors arrived. We probably couldn't afford one anyway, particularly if he was smart enough to join the union.

agency with more than 100,000 employees and a $160 billion budget—the pale-faced CEO turned to me to ask earnestly, as he was leaving, "What did I do wrong?"

The CEO was Geoff Freeman, at the time newly appointed as CEO of the Grocery Manufacturers Association (GMA). Prior to his arrival, GMA had endured several tumultuous years, not least of all due to its engagement on genetically modified food disclosure legislation across the country and in Washington. Shortly after taking the helm, Mr. Freeman led GMA's relaunch as the Consumer Brands Association. He was polished, prepared, and had led another large trade association for several years before being tapped to be the lead voice for America's $2.1 trillion food, beverage, and consumer products industry. For him, a discussion with the nation's top agriculture official would have been almost perfunctory, and indeed it had been placed on the Secretary's calendar largely as a "get to know" meeting.[2]

The Secretary, a broad shouldered two-term governor and cabinet Secretary known for his general congeniality, also possessed a keen sense of when to eschew the "go along to get along" personality. His "aw shucks" persona could be mesmerizing, but Secretary Perdue played for keeps in the policy arena. Secretary Perdue was wise enough to know that farmers needed allies, and on this day he was looking for some.

In the Secretary's view (and mine), food manufacturers were in a unique position to educate the consumer. As Secretary Perdue pressed in the meeting for food manufacturers to step up and use their unique relationships with consumers to push back on fears about everything from genetically modified foods to hollow metrics

2. Such a meeting was longer than the fly-bys that we as staffers referred to as "meet and greets" on the Secretary's schedule, but not nearly as in depth as "policy time" with key staff members and policy experts, where issues like this one were often discussed at length.

of sustainability, it became clear that GMA was determined to leave its advocacy battles in the past and exit the arena.

The Secretary's goal was to press food manufacturers for a more palatable commitment to the noble task of pushing back against unfounded consumer fears and anxiety, particularly when they undermined technology or methodology that held the promise of responsibly increasing farmers' productivity gains. In short, Secretary Perdue wanted the food manufacturers enlisted in the fight. As became clear in the meeting, the goal of the trade association that represented those manufacturers, on the other hand, was to stay out of it. Secretary Perdue was, politely, stunned by what seemed to be the food industry's about-face or—maybe—surrender.

Truth be told, the CEO had done nothing wrong. But the conversation he had just had with the Secretary epitomized the challenges attendant to the growing tensions between those who grow our food and those just outside—and in some instances completely outside—of the farming profession. In this case, the tension manifested itself between a wise and well-heeled farmer-leader who happened to occupy the most significant agriculture policy role in the world and a newly minted and accomplished food manufacturing sector leader, but that is just one example you will read in this book.

By design, the meeting should have been just another cordial discussion. After all, those who produce our food—called farmers throughout this book—and those who process, package, and market it, obviously need each other. Even more obviously, they both need consumers and are generally not aligned to be in direct competition for them.

Unfortunately for the Secretary and the CEO, the tectonic plates of the farmer and food system lithosphere were set in motion long before this sit-down, and not because of anything either of them had done individually. This eruption was simply one more emanation of the very real tensions that are now shaping the future of food and agriculture around the world, and particularly in the United States.

THE INSIDERS

On one side—represented generally here by the Secretary's point of view—are the women and men who grow our food. Ag insiders. They work hard. They are honest. They are proud of their contribution to food security. And most of them do not do it solely for the money (a fact that many an ag lender has had to meticulously demonstrate to them, sometimes heartbreakingly, over the years).

Having been around a few farmers, I think it is more than fair to say that most would recoil at the notion that something is inherently wrong with the way food is being grown in the United States, much less the increasingly common view that the very system that supplies the safest, most abundant, economical food supply in the world is somehow "broken." They view skeptically any suggestion that consumers have adequate grounds for being dissatisfied with the way the system operates, particularly as it relates to the actual practice of farming.

Farmers point repeatedly to the hypothesis that if consumers were just more educated about how agriculture works, they would come around to their point of view. In many a farmer's mind, consumers' snobby demands for trendy labels that villainize the latest scientific breakthroughs are counterproductive. This is precisely why Secretary Perdue was so interested in teaming up with food manufacturers. Farmers' go-to argument has been that most of what food manufacturers want to slap on the wrapper is not educational at all. Instead, and they are right about this, it often capitalizes on consumers' ignorance and fear. Trigger words that hype the notion that only a select few farmers are true stewards of God's creation are, to farmer insiders, a sign that outside influences on the food system are at best based on ignorance, and at worst driven by sinister motivations. They walk away, as the kids say on text, SMH—shaking my head (or their heads, in this case).

The Outsiders

On the other side—represented in this particular conversation by the hesitancy of the trade association CEO—are the foodies and other ag ecosystem "outsiders." They did not grow up on farms, have never grown and canned their own produce, do not derive their income from agriculture, and most likely do not have any close family members that do. Some of them view the agriculture and food enterprise as one that is in a sad state of decline, with its lacquered-on pesticides, blatant animal abuse, exploitation of workers, and decimation of the environment. They see "big ag" and "big food" as a mission field ripe for conversion.

As I'll make clear in this book, the point here is not that this particular CEO or his trade association hold (or do not hold) the view that the food system is broken. Nor that food manufacturers are, themselves, outsiders. But the CEO and his member companies do have to interface directly with consumers and thought leaders who are listening to the outsiders and who have concluded that something must change. Generally, their dilemma is that they are more interested in selling to their customers than arguing with them. Which I'm sure their shareholders appreciate.

These outsiders sometimes go so far as to excuse the actions of individual farmers, believing that such farmers have been, bless their hearts, duped by what they refer to as the overgrown, over-mechanized, concentrated, corporate apparatus that has become the modern food system. But make no mistake. To them, much of the food system is broken, if not entirely corrupt and irredeemable.

Food system outsiders—a term I use in this book to describe the many who have taken up the call to arms of rewiring the circuitry of the food chain—appear to be the knights in shining armor here. (I will describe these outsiders further in Chapter 2.) They and their eclectic foodie brethren—as the term foodie is more traditionally understood—are well-funded and well-organized. They dominate modern media platforms and intellectual debate fora. They are moving the market. And food companies are listening to them. So are investors and politicians.

THE DISCONNECT

How can these radically different views of modern agriculture coexist? In one world, farmers and ag groups pat themselves on the back for a job incredibly well done. To them, their practices are sustainable, their treatment of the environment respectable, their recognition of the dignity of workers and animals admirable, and their contribution to society unmistakable. In a parallel universe, there are those who have made it their mission to dismantle a system they see as broken, polluting, collusive, irresponsible, and politically entrenched in its own self-propagation.

Perhaps a better question is, why should you care about this disconnect? There are numerous disconnects and disagreements in society on a wide variety of issues. Why in the world would someone write a book about this?

It's Personal

This is deeply personal for me. I grew up on a family-owned Century Farm in Southeast North Carolina.[3] Decades before I was born, my father quit an hourly job after missing out on a promotion and instantly became a full-time farmer. My mother left her steady-income teaching job to become the farm bookkeeper, talent development organizer, and field crew leader.

Growing up, I chased hogs through the woods with a stick (only when they had gotten out, which was often), threw hay bales *up* into the barn loft, and could see and smell the permanent stain of tobacco gum on my hands long after I was out of the field. My eldest brother, Willi, received an agronomy degree before returning home to take over the family farm, which he has done admirably. My elder brother Steve is a Farm Credit Express guru and can rattle off the names of every farm equipment dealer in Eastern North Carolina, with a strong likelihood that he can give a recommendation of a nearby barbecue restaurant, too.

We are an ag family, and we are proud of it.

I was active in 4-H and FFA and will forever be indebted for having the opportunity to serve as a National FFA Officer. While FFA offers personal growth opportunities in many different ways, I am most fond of its role in helping farm kids and rural students poke their heads up a little higher than they would have without the experience. The opportunity to stand up tall enough (or to be propped up enough) to look beyond the edges of the tobacco fields and hog farm of my youth literally changed the trajectory of my life. It also allowed me to meet thousands of other inspiring farm kids and mentors along the way. I studied agricultural education at one of the nation's best land-grant institutions, obtained my law degree from a

3. North Carolina's Century Farm program honors farms a particular family has owned or operated for more than one hundred years, a distinction that applies to only 3-4 percent of farms in the state.

top-tier law school, and have even had the fortune of returning there to teach agriculture and food law to extraordinarily sharp students.

I have listened to and worked with thousands of farmers not just in North Carolina but across the country. Some on their best days, some on their worst. I've arranged for them to meet with state legislators and state directors and commissioners of agriculture, U.S. House Members and Senators, the Secretary of Agriculture, and yes, even the President of the United States. I've listened intently in those conversations, including those in the Roosevelt Room of the West Wing and those in the back of a Ford Explorer riding around a pig farm. I have worked closely with the leadership of their trade associations, learning the intricacies of issues as broad as international trade and as specific as ethanol blend walls. I've even had a conversation in the Oval Office that led to salvaging agriculture's largest trade deal.

At the same time, I've toured not just farms but food-processing plants and phosphate fertilizer mines. Taken dignitaries and students through processing facilities. Met with food aid leaders from around the world in Djibouti and Mozambique. Talked to trade officials from Europe, Mexico, South America, and the Pacific Rim. Debated the Common Agriculture Policy with farm organization leaders in Sweden. I've listened as leaders from food companies and their representatives discuss everything from FDA labeling requirements to their knowledge of the "bite" needed to make sure plant-based chicken nuggets meet the needs of discerning fifth graders. I now work for the NC Chamber promoting a business climate that we believe makes my home state one of the best places in the world to do business—including agribusiness.

In the fullest of disclosure, I believe that the entire food ecosystem, including farmers and food companies, have given us much to be proud of. Secretary of Agriculture Sonny Perdue, whom I had the honor of working closely with for more than two years, was always fond of saying, "When man has no food, he has one problem; when man has plenty of food, he has plenty of problems."[4] The point was not lost on me. We have a luxury here in the United States that is not available to many around the world. Because of the efficiency and effectiveness of our farmers and others in the food system, we can seek to improve that system with our mouths and bellies full.

These personal experiences have also given me a vantage point to see the bigger field. For farmers, the alarming thing about the critiques lobbed by those outside the food chain is not just that those critiques are substantively at odds with farmers' views (and many of my own). It's that those who hold these contrarian views seem to be increasingly louder and more effective at convincing others that the system needs some sort of massive overhaul. In other words, the volume and power of the outsider seems to be growing, and that of the farmer seems to be waning. Frighteningly, the result might very well be farmers forced by the market, government policy, or cultural pressure to adopt practices that have no measurable benefit and that actually make us *more* food insecure.

It Should Be Personal for You

The match is set. If you identify more closely with sitting on a tractor than you do with selecting which items you want in the food box delivered to your front porch, your ability to influence how the food system works is likely in a spiraling decline. Suppliers generally have to follow their customers, and in this paradigm, the farmer is the supplier. Sellers do not typically set the final terms of a deal unilaterally, and the trends in both food policy and expenditure of the food dollar bear out this observation.

4. He also said one time that "sometimes when people do not see the light, you have to make them feel the heat." You just don't get sage leadership advice like that from people who don't eat boiled peanuts.

To be clear, this text is not about fearmongering amongst the aggies. Our nation needs our proud farmers now as much as we ever have.[5] And without question your author identifies more closely with them than he does with folks who drink kombucha and buy GMO-free flax seed crackers. He certainly identifies more closely with the farmer than he does with the academic activist who has never heartbreakingly disced under a field of perfectly good produce or smelled soybeans destroyed by floodwater or hail.

But we cannot ignore the real drivers behind Costco growing its own chickens, Walmart and Kroger making their own milk while stocking milk made from things that never lactate, and much of the venture capital in production agriculture coming from individuals quite distant from the fields of my childhood.[6]

This book is also not a call to arms. It is, however, what a former boss of mine who had a career in consulting before becoming a state house speaker and U.S. senator would call a "level set." A "sitrep." An assessment of the current state of play and where we are headed, what to watch for, and what can be ignored.

Many of the agriculture community's previous efforts to turn the hearts and minds of our critics have not prevented us from arriving at this crossroads, so why would those efforts miraculously start working next week? Hoping that sincerely held consumer beliefs, market forces, and policy and political trends are merely fads or random voices that will eventually be drowned out by the roar of tractor motors and local community dinners attended mostly by

5. The world needs them too, but not as much as those of us in agriculture like to think. "American farmers feed the world" and other exaggerations are discussed in the closing chapter of this book.

6. "To keep the $4.99 rotisserie chicken and its cultlike status, Costco participated in a first-of-its-kind experiment. It built its own chicken-processing facility to fully integrate the growing and processing of its poultry supply chain." Bob Sims, "Costco's Road to Rotisserie," *Meat + Poultry,* December 6, 2019, *https://www.meatpoultry.com/articles/22311-costcos-rotisserie-chicken-plant-proof-of-concept* and Jacob Bunge and Jaewon Kang, "Walmart, Kroger Bottle Their Own Milk and Shake Up American Dairy Industry," The *Wall Street Journal,* July 27, 2020, *https://www.wsj.com/articles/walmart-kroger-bottle-their-own-milk-and-shake-up-american-dairy-industry-11595872190.*

farmers is not really a plan. This is true even if those beliefs, market forces, and policy trends are not really in the long-term best interest of the food system. They are not going away on their own.

While public views of farmers and agriculture are overwhelmingly positive,[7] a fact farmers are often surprised to learn, that same public can hold the view that they want more from their food and, apparently, their food system. Indeed, consumers may romanticize farmers in the abstract, but the most frightening observation I have extrapolated from the data is that they may do so only because they do not understand who the modern farmer is. Stated differently, the disconnect between consumers loving farmers, but not loving "big ag" and "big food," is largely premised on their ignorance about which farmers are feeding the world. Here's a hint: it's not always the ones with pumpkin patches and chickens grown on the outside. I'm still torn about whether we should tell them.

This book is about recognizing these tensions, considering their sources, and having an intellectually honest conversation about understanding and positioning for how to counteract or adjust for them. It is no longer enough to criticize, roll our eyes at the outsiders, say the same things we have said before more loudly, and cue Paul Harvey.

Who Needs to Hear This?

I'm convinced that when someone begins a social media post with "I'm not sure who needs to hear this," it is highly unlikely that the people who do hear it are the ones who need to. Hopefully that is not the case with this book.

7. "For the first time in Gallup's 20 years of tracking Americans' views of various business and industry sectors, farming and agriculture is the clear leader." Lydia Saad, "Farming Rises, Sports Tumbles in U.S. Industry Ratings," Gallup, September 8, 2020, *https://news.gallup.com/poll/319256/farming-rises-sports-tumbles-industry-ratings.aspx.*

My target audience includes individuals who work inside the agriculture and agribusiness industry and who want to continue being the predominant force that shapes it. The overarching goal is to examine the contemporary rise of critiques and challenges to our system of agriculture, and ultimately the calls for its wholesale deconstruction. Along the way, I will point to some of the most hyperbolic criticisms of agriculture—the fad I refer to in Chapter 2 as "Humpty Dumptyism." I note the cultural allure and significance of food and, by extension, agriculture in Chapter 3. That sets up a discussion about the latest consumer preferences and trends (chapters 4 and 5), a topic that will no doubt be familiar to many agricultural thought leaders, but unfortunately is generally the beginning and the end of what most agriculturalists think about when they think about outsiders changing the future of farming and food.

Going beyond consumer trends, in Chapter 6, I examine the deluge of outside investment in agriculture with an eye toward deciphering why our industry has become the favored landing site for socially motivated investment. For years, we've lamented our waning political prowess, so I try to investigate those claims in Chapter 7. Spoiler alert: our laments are well placed.

What lawyer could write a book without talking about the importance of lawyers? Chapter 8 draws attention to the outsiders' use of legal leverage to reshape the industry. American agriculture will feel more and more the pressure of its decades-long foray into international markets, and you will be surprised at the chess moves being made by some of our competitors around the world. They are chronicled in Chapter 9.

The goal of Chapter 10 is to demonstrate how some of the anti-agriculture narratives get their wings and eventually fly. Much of agriculture's public-affairs strategy seems to remain focused on the symptoms of a less complimentary media environment, without grasping—much less addressing—the root cause of the message onslaught of our detractors.

Chapter 11 shares my personal reflections on how we got here, mainly through the lens of larger cultural trends and sentiments. Finally, Chapter 12 offers humble thoughts on where we go from here.

Who Is Winning?

Back to that meeting in the Secretary's outer office.

It is a huge room. Through the years, thousands of individuals have passed under those chandeliers, been photographed while standing by the massive ceremonial desk, or sat proudly in one of the burgundy swivel chairs ringing the oversized oak conference table. While Secretary Perdue occupied the office, dozens of visitors commented on the size of the elk head mounted above the couch that nobody ever sat on,[8] while hundreds more gazed at it but did not comment because they did not actually know what it was. Agricultural leaders and bureaucrats alike often scanned the room during meetings there, hoping to take in the sanctity of that place where so many agricultural issues have been debated.

As far as rooms in one-hundred-year-old government buildings are concerned, this one has hosted its fair share of consequential conversations. This was the room where big ideas came to flourish, or to die. Sell it to the Secretary or do not ever mention it again. Decision row.

As it turns out, the biggest question facing the food system was teed up for discussion on that very day. Would the trade association take up the fight on behalf of farmers to convince those outside the food system that some of their ideas would actually take the world

8. Perhaps afraid the elk might fall on them, which was probably not an unreasonable fear.

backward, or would they cave to glib consumer demands and whims in search of next quarter's earnings target?

There was no resolution. Both sides left frustrated.

The way that meeting played out almost perfectly encapsulates the ongoing struggle over who will call the shots regarding food in the future. Farmers are tempted to lash out or throw punches, or to scoffingly shake their heads at what they believe is completely unjustified meddling with their livelihoods. Food companies lay low, sometimes pacifying the calls for activism one way or the other, hoping they can continue to stay ahead of the next consumer boycott while simultaneously marketing themselves using the face of their most photogenic farmer supplier.

In the meantime, the outsiders, including foodies and TED Talkers, run circles around all of us, spraying the public with relentless artillery fired from the perch of diversified media portals, social influence channels, and even parts of academia and the church.

The food system outsiders are gaining ground. And they weren't even in the room.

CHAPTER TWO

The Humpty Dumpty Megaphone

Have you ever paused and asked, "Where is all of this coming from?" "Who are these people?" "Do they live in some sort of alternative universe?" "How can anyone who benefits from the bounty of food available in this country possibly believe that the most pressing thing they could be working on is fixing the food system?"

I myself have wondered whether there is some sort of underground army that recruits soldiers for the foodie revolution using clandestine techniques, complete with oaths of office and fingerprinting. What would the test for joining the brigade include? Would providing a picture of the inside of your refrigerator be a requirement? Perhaps that's why those new refrigerators have cameras inside them.

As it turns out, there is. Sort of. The foodie movement has many authors, generals, and plebes. As noted in Chapter 1, these players operate largely outside the farming and food space—meaning they prefer to tweak and critique the system without putting their own capital at risk in any form of farming or food production operation. When they do try their own hands at food production, they frequently fail. They then blame—you guessed it—the "broken" system. They nonetheless know all of the ag and food system's deepest, darkest problems, and you can "click here" to support their work to rectify them if you wish.

According to Steve Striffler, the author of the 2005 book *Chicken: The Dangerous Transformation of America's Favorite Food*, food system activists generally fall into one of two camps: those who believe we must confront the conventional system and reform it, and those who believe we need to build alternatives. He points out that each of these strategies presents different jumping-off points for how activists enter the debate. Make no mistake, Mr. Striffler believes those who assess the system as some combination of immoral, unhealthy, unfair, or unsustainable have the better arguments. In fact, he's disappointed food activists have not been able to be more successful. Striffler connects their lack of success mainly to the mistake of pointing to the food industry when the real culprit is capitalism.[9] Watch for the dichotomy espoused by activists in the following paragraphs, as some call for reform and others for wholesale disruption.

A Way with Words

I like YouTube. I watch it mostly when I'm exercising, as it gives me something to look at besides the blinking dots on the treadmill that tell me to punish myself more vigorously. YouTube is full of informative talks and inspirational videos. YouTube is also brimming

9. Steve Striffler, "Food Activism: A Critical History," in *Food Fights*, pp. 61–76.

with scathing critiques of our food system, most of which would be immediately addressed if everyone just took up arms and "voted differently with their food dollar."

Take, for example, the teachings of Josh Tetrick. Tetrick is the CEO of JUST, Inc., a company that has developed a plant-based egg substitute derived from the mung bean. Tetrick played football at West Virginia University, attended law school at the University of Michigan, and earned a Fulbright Scholarship that allowed him to work in Africa. In his TED Talk entitled "The Future of Food," Tetrick says within the first minute and thirty seconds that "food, guys, is a broken system."[10] A few seconds later he stakes the claim out a little further: "Food is broken through and through."

Raj Patel is a research professor at the University of Texas and a senior research associate at Rhodes University in South Africa. He touts educational credentials from the University of Oxford, the London School of Economics, and Cornell.[11] Patel is also a food system reform author, having penned *Stuffed and Starved: The Hidden Battle for the World Food System* in 2012.

The quotes that can be pulled from Patel's lecture "The World That Food Made," filmed at Arizona State University in late 2018, are so numerous you should explore them for yourself.[12] For example, "There's no such thing as a sustainable food industry," and that, in 2017, "the industry that killed more [indigenous] people than any other was agribusiness." He continues with the cold-blooded murder analogy: "There's a death toll associated with this cheap food, which the food industry knows all too well."[13]

10. TEDx Talks, "The Future of Food: Josh Tetrick at TEDxEdmonton," YouTube video, 1:21, posted June 23, 2013, *https://www.youtube.com/watch?v=QVTkdpfeb8A*.

11. Ironically, a land-grant university.

12. Global Institute of Sustainability and Innovation, "'The World That Food Made' with Raj Patel," YouTube video, posted November 21, 2018, *https://www.youtube.com/watch?v=u9IYVO9HVRo*.

13. My favorite of Patel's illustrations is his belief that in hundreds of years, archaeologists will find large repositories of chicken bones in the present era's rock formations, given

You get the point. But we can't stop there.

A 2019 article in the science journal *Nature* bears the headline "Fix the Broken Food System in Three Steps."[14] Its authors include Guido Schmidt-Traub, executive director of the United Nations' Sustainable Development Solutions Network in Paris, Michael Obersteiner, program director of Ecosystems Services and Management at the International Institute for Applied Systems Analysis in Laxenburg, Austria, and Aline Mosnier, a colleague of Dr. Schmidt-Traub's and more specifically the scientific director of FABLE, an acronym for the international Food, Agriculture, Biodiversity, Land-Use, and Energy consortium.

These are extraordinarily bright researchers who hold very influential roles in the international food system discussion. Here's their take on world agriculture:

> *Land use and food production are not meeting people's needs. Agriculture destroys forests and biodiversity, squanders water and releases one-quarter of global greenhouse-gas emissions. Yet one-third of food is wasted, 800 million people remain undernourished, 2 billion are deficient in micronutrients, and obesity is on the rise. These figures will worsen as the planet warms, soils degrade and the global population grows, urbanizes and consumes more.*

Well, that's uplifting. About the only word they failed to use was deplorable. Fear not, though, because at least they know the three steps to rectify all the food system's shortcomings.

---

the more than twenty billion chickens that supply us with everything from chicken tenders to fingers and paws. I don't think anyone has explained to Mr. Patel what exactly chicken meal is or the action-verb nature of the word "rendered."

14. Guido Schmidt-Traub, Michael Obersteiner and Aline Mosnier, "Fix the Broken Food System in Three Steps," *Nature*, May 8, 2019, *https://www.nature.com/articles/d41586-019-01420-2*.

Their views have good company. The title of another 2019 article, this one at Climate Home News, reads, "Our food system is broken. Here's how we fix it."[15] The author is Paul Polman, the former CEO of Unilever. Mr. Polman is also the former chair of the Food and Land Use Coalition and the International Chamber of Commerce, and former vice-chair of the UN Global Compact. Again, not an uninformed speaker, and no intellectual lightweight.

Mr. Polman, who has a Master's of Arts in Economics and an MBA in Finance and International Marketing from the University of Cincinnati, along with a couple of honorary doctoral degrees, points to a plan of action to "transform our broken food system to deliver more nutritious food, help avert runaway climate change and biodiversity loss, and improve economic opportunity and livelihoods for farmers." His premise is that we have the power to correct the broken food system, we just need the courage to do it.

Not surprisingly, Hollywood has its fair share of proponents for reforming the food system. Alec Baldwin, for example, has stated that "our current food systems are causing great harm to our planet, as well as our health."[16]

Some call for transformation. Others for reform. Still others want to see the current system dismantled. An official with the United Nations' International Fund for Agricultural Development has said we need a "revolution." Jyotsna Puri, an associate vice president of IFAD, wrote the following in a September 2021 op-ed for the Hill that "It is clear that we need a revolution of our food systems: the way we grow, harvest, process, transport, sell and consume our foods. A change so dramatic that previous versions of food systems

---

15. Paul Polman, "Our Food System Is Broken. Here's How We Fix It," Climate Home News, July 11, 2019, *https://www.climatechangenews.com/2019/11/07/food-system-broken-heres-fix/*.

16. Charlotte Pointing, "Why Alec Baldwin Really Wants You to Eat More Vegan Food," *LIVEKINDLY*, December 15, 2020, https://www.livekindly.co/alec-baldwin-more-vegan-food/.

are unrecognizable."[17] The title of her piece references the "four steps" needed to bring about such revolution.

I keep waiting for someone to offer all of this for $19.99 and throw in an extra spatula if you order in the next thirty minutes.

You might think I cherry-picked these examples, which appear largely focused on the state of the international food system, and that homegrown, American views of the domestic food system are undoubtedly different. If so, you'd be wrong.

Food Tank, which refers to itself as "the think tank for food," begins its "About Us" page with this sentence: "Our food system is broken."[18]

The Environmental Working Group, which annually publishes a "Dirty Dozen" shopping guide to "pesticides in produce," attracts the eyeballs of millions. It's genius. I typically read it, and I try to enjoy one of the items that they suggest is so toxic at the same time. The organization further notes: "Pesticides are sprayed on millions of acres every year and some of them end up on your food. Our broken farm subsidy system encourages over production of the wrong food."[19]

Laurie J. Beyranevand is the director of the Center for Agriculture and Food Systems at Vermont Law School, and Emily Broad Leib is a clinical professor of law at Harvard Law School. They are the lead authors of the 2017 report entitled "The Urgent Call for a U.S. National Food Strategy," which was updated again in October of 2020. From the introduction[20] of the 2020 publication:

---

17. Jyotsna Puri, "4 Steps to Make the Global Food System More Sustainable," the Hill, September 21, 2021, *https://thehill.com/opinion/energy-environment/572768-4-steps-to-make-the-global-food-system-more-sustainable*.

18. "About Food Tank," About, foodtank, last modified August 23, 2021, *https://foodtank.com/about*.

19. "Dirty Dozen," Dirty Dozen, The Environmental Working Group, last modified March 29, 2021, *https://www.ewg.org/foodnews/dirty-dozen.php*. and "Food," Areas of Focus, The Environmental Working Group, last modified March 29, 2021, https://www.ewg.org/areas-focus.

20. Emily Broad Leib and Laurie Beyranevand, "The Urgent Call for a U.S. National Food Strategy (An Update to the Blueprint, 2020)," Food Strategy Blueprint. *https://*

> *The United States continues to face concurrent and interrelated crises of food-related inequality, diet-related disease, and environmental and climate disruption. While the inequalities, challenges, and inconsistencies endemic to the U.S. food system have long been recognized, the COVID-19 pandemic exacerbated these issues and shone a spotlight on them. . . .*
>
> *Food and agriculture account for 5.4 percent of the American economy, contributing more than $1 trillion to the U.S. gross domestic product ("GDP"). The food system also employs 11 percent of the U.S. workforce, and the entirety of the U.S. population has an economic stake in the food system, as we all participate as consumers.* **However, the food system fails to meet our nation's most important and basic needs in a variety of ways.** *[Emphasis in original.]*

Note the irony of the problem of simultaneously having too much food (references to diet-related disease and obesity) and too little food at the same time. This is actually now a mainstream argument regularly lobbed at the food system. That its bad characteristics are laden with efficiency (and free enterprise) and its good ones are underdeveloped. It is the system itself—and certainly not consumers—that have driven us to where we are. The Pennington Biomedical Research Center advertises compassionately: "It's not what you're eating, it's what you're being fed."[21]

---

foodstrategyblueprint.org/wp-content/uploads/2020/10/food-strategy-report-update-2020.pdf.

21. Pennington Biomedical Research Center, "Science Characterizes the Current State of America as 'Obecity, USA,'" Pennington Biomedical Research Center, Louisiana State University, May 6, 2021, https://www.pbrc.edu/news/media/2021/Obecity-USA.aspx.

Beyranevand and Broad Leib were even more dire in their contribution to the Hill,[22] with particular attention paid to the argument that COVID-19 had not exacerbated the brokenness of the food system as much as it had merely unmasked it:

> *America's food system has long been plagued by massive inefficiencies and injustices. They just weren't quite so visible to all before now. Soaring rates of food insecurity, the exploitation of food workers, massive volumes of food waste, widespread nutritional deficiencies leading to alarming rates of diet related disease, the challenging economics of farming and disproportionate harm to underserved and Black, Indigenous and people of color (BIPOC) communities—all of these existed at near-crisis levels before the coronavirus first infected a single human. The virus and resulting public health measures simply brought these issues to the front burner and turned them up to a rolling boil.*
>
> *The reasons that COVID-19 had our food system on the brink of collapse are the same ones that have allowed these inequalities and failures to persist for decades.*

Beyranevand has plenty of platforms from which to make this claim, as she is, according to her biography on the Vermont Law School website, a member of the Food and Drug Law Institute and Georgetown Law School's *Food and Drug Law Journal* Editorial Advisory Board, was a founding member of the Academy of Food

22. Laurie Beyranevand and Emily Broad Leib, "Our Food System Is Broken—There's a Blueprint to Fix It," the Hill, January 21, 2021, *https://thehill.com/opinion/energy-environment/535070-our-food-system-is-broken-theres-a-blueprint-to-fix-it#bottom-story-socials.*

Law and Policy, and serves as the Chair Elect of the Agriculture and Food Law Section of the American Association of Law Schools. Broad Leib is the founder of Harvard Law School's Food Law and Policy Clinic, which is devoted to "providing clients with legal and policy solutions to address the health, economic, and environmental challenges facing our food system."[23] These two scholars' indictments of the food system are one thing, but consider the weight added to their arguments by virtue of their positions within the upper echelon of the educational academy.[24]

Our elected leaders make similar claims. In April of 2021, Senator Cory Booker said the following while speaking to the National Action Network's national convention:

> *In addition to a hunger crisis, we face a second great crisis, one of nutrition insecurity, where too many Americans are overfed, but undernourished, and we continue to pour massive federal subsidies into a system that is literally making us sick. . . .*
>
> *The American food system is broken, and it is killing us. The American food system is working against nearly everyone it touches—it is hurting urban communities and rural communities; farmers and farm workers. And it is deeply dangerous to our most vulnerable communities. The only winners in this system are the massive, consolidated multinational*

23. "Emily M. Broad Leib," Faculty, Harvard Law School, *https://hls.harvard.edu/faculty/directory/11185/BroadLeib/* (n/d).

24. I once heard that Harvard graduates were reluctant to mention their credentials because doing so could create awkward silence. Such a graduate would therefore sometimes shy away from dropping what they called the "H-bomb." I doubt the Manhattan Project architects would appreciate the reference. I reticently agreed it sounded about right, and I do appreciate this Cambridge-taught level of humility directed toward the rest of us hillbillies. After all, it is written that no person can handle looking directly into the face of God.

> *corporations that dominate our food industry and too often dictate food policy.*[25]

Here again, the argument is that the system is both too good at providing the wrong nutrition and terribly bad at supplying the right nourishment at the same time. One could argue that Senator Booker, who is a member of the Senate Agriculture Committee and the Chair of the Subcommittee on Food and Nutrition, Specialty Crops, Organics, and Research, was actually more measured in his prepared remarks for NAN than he was in an exclusive September 2020 interview with the *Guardian*. There, he stated that the food system was "savagely" broken, which is apparently worse than just being ordinarily broken.[26]

Senator Booker fingered the greatest contributor to the savagely broken system as the faceless, multinational corporations who abuse workers, communities, and the environment.

> *I don't think most Americans realize that the way we raise animals is such a betrayal of the heritage of our grandparents. I don't think they realize that . . . these big companies like Smithfield and Cargill and others have our American farmers now living like sharecroppers in constant debt, forced to follow their rules. I've watched the suffering in North Carolina*

25. Cory Booker, "At National Action Network Convention, Booker Raises Alarm on America's Broken Food System and the Nutrition Crisis Endangering Communities of Color," Cory Booker, April 14, 2021, *https://www.booker.senate.gov/news/press/at-national-action-network-convention-booker-raises-alarm-on-americas-broken-food-system-and-the-nutrition-crisis-endangering-communities-of-color*.

26. I remember driving over a piece of irrigation pipe as a kid working on the farm. It was destroyed. Once I realized what I had done, my most immediate dilemma was how I might pull it out from under the truck, which would have been extraordinarily difficult without backing up or running the second set of wheels over the same piece of pipe. I chose to back up over it, meaning I had now run over it twice, albeit the second time intentionally. I suppose you could say I broke it the first time, but the second time, I broke it savagely.

> *of minority communities who live around Cafos*[27] *and can no longer breathe their air . . . and I've seen workers in the meatpacking plants and how dangerous those plants are.*
>
> *Everybody is losing in this system—except for the massive corporations that have taken over the American food system.*[28]

The Senator's call to action continued:

> *What's motivating me is that I think we need to really sound the alarm in America. There are so many crises [that relate] to public health, from global warming to economic justice to humane treatment of animals. What should not be surprising is that a senator is taking this on. What should be more surprising is that we as a country have not seen this broken food system, especially after a Covid crisis, which has so exposed the fragility of the American food system. The real question is why isn't Congress as a whole moving to address this massive threat to public health?*

To paraphrase: it is so broken that my colleagues don't even see it! The *Guardian* hailed the Senator's bravery in tackling this issue while nearby click-bait beckoned me to read even more about the

27. CAFO is an acronym for "concentrated animal feeding operations," and is typically used by ag system outsiders to refer derogatorily to large animal production operations. It is more and more common to see it as written here—as a formal word, as opposed to as an acronym. I'm surprised they didn't figure out a way to throw in a reference to the "corporate" business organization status of many of these farms, so that the acronym would actually be CCAFOs.

28. Lisa Elaine Held, "'A savagely broken food system': Cory Booker wants radical reform . . . now," the *Guardian,* September 15, 2020, *https://www.theguardian.com/environment/2020/sep/15/a-savagely-broken-food-system-cory-booker-wants-radical-reform-now.*

atrocities taking place on our farms. Fortunately for him, there are others in Congress willing to attend to the Humpty Dumpty food system, including Senator Elizabeth Warren of Massachusetts.

Senator Warren joined Senator Booker in introducing the "Farm System Reform Act of 2021," and upon its filing issued a press release panning the "hyper consolidation of our livestock and meat industry," the "near collapse of the supply chain" during COVID, and . . . wait for it . . . the "broken system" that supplies our food.

The Senator posits that this broken system was not created by "inevitable market forces but rather comes directly from the influence that multinational meatpackers—who continued to make record profits during the pandemic—have over federal farm policy."[29] The former Harvard Law School professor and former Republican staked out her views on how to reform American agriculture during her campaign for the presidency by touting her "New Farm Economy Plan." She sought to replace our "government's failed approach," adding quickly that "our agriculture markets are badly broken."[30]

One food and farming industry critic went so far as to say that the broken food system is so broken it is not even worth fixing. AJ Albrecht, the director of government affairs at Mercy for Animals, which promotes a vegan diet and states that its mission is to "construct a compassionate food system,"[31] published an article on Salon.com in 2020 with the title "The U.S. food system is broken—and we shouldn't try to fix it."[32]

---

29. Elizabeth Warren, "Warren Joins Booker in Reintroducing Bill to Reform Farm System With Support From Farm, Labor, Environment, Public Health, Faith Based and Animal Welfare Groups," Elizabeth Warren, July 13, 2021, *https://www.warren.senate.gov/newsroom/press-releases/07/21/2021/warren-joins-booker-in-reintroducing-bill-to-reform-farm-system-with-support-from-farm-labor-environment-public-health-faith-based-and-animal-welfare-groups.*

30. "A New Farm Economy," Plans, Elizabeth Warren, last modified August 7, 2019, *https://elizabethwarren.com/plans/new-farm-economy.*

31. "Mercy for Animals," Home, Mercy for Animals, last modified November 19, 2021, *https://mercyforanimals.org/.*

32. AJ Albrecht, "The U.S. Food System Is Broken—And We Shouldn't Try to Fix It," Salon, June 13, 2020, *https://www.salon.com/2020/06/13/*

The subhead reads, "The federal government shouldn't be trying to salvage our broken food system—we need a new one." Albrecht is also, by the way, the chair of the American Bar Association's Tort Trial and Insurance Practice Section's Animal Law Committee.[33]

There are institutes, too. The Good Food Institute claims on their website that "current meat production is unsustainable and inefficient. It is a key driver of climate change, environmental degradation, and antibiotic-resistant disease."[34]

In other words, it is going to take all the king's horses and all the king's men to put the Humpty Dumpty food system back together again. The most difficult part of chronicling just how widespread the claim is that the food system is broken is knowing where to stop.[35]

And finally, there's my friend Sarah Mock. Sarah and I are proof two people can agree to disagree agreeably, as long as it helps sell books, and I have to give it to her—she has a way with words that few other people do.[36] For example, her recently published book is entitled *Farm (and Other F Words): The Rise and Fall of the Small Family Farm*. I wholeheartedly recommend you read it.

In a November 2018 Medium post, Sarah opens with, "If you ever find yourself at a dinner party, trapped in a conversation about

---

the-us-food-system-is-broken–and-we-shouldnt-try-to-fix-it_partner/.

33. I'm starting to wonder why there are so many lawyers who moonlight as food system critics. I once saw, while working in a law firm, an ad for a doormat that read, "A Lawyer and a Normal Person Live Here." I didn't buy it.

34. "About GFI," About, gfi, last modified May 18, 2021, *https://gfi.org/about/*.

35. Miriam Nelson, "The Pandemic Revealed Our Food System Is Broken. We Can Fix It," the *Boston Globe,* March 2, 2021, *https://www.bostonglobe.com/2021/03/02/magazine/pandemic-revealed-our-food-system-is-broken-we-can-fix-it/*. and Viktoria de Bourbon de Parme, "What Companies Can Do to Fix Our Broken Food System," *Reuters Events,* January 5, 2021, *https://www.reutersevents.com/sustainability/what-companies-can-do-fix-our-broken-food-system*. and Tamar Haspel, "10 Things We Should Do to Fix Our Broken Food System," the *Washington Post,* December 28, 2015, *https://www.washingtonpost.com/lifestyle/food/10-things-we-should-do-to-fix-our-broken-food-system/2015/12/28/ea720336-a8f7-11e5-9b92-dea7cd4b1a4d_story.html*. and Emiko Terazono, "Is Our Food System Broken?,"*Financial Times,* May 21, 2020, *https://www.ft.com/content/89b7d0c1-cb11-495e-a9bb-4bba5c05816c*.

36. I also have to give it to her that she probably will sell more books than me.

food or agriculture, it's very fashionable to say something like: 'The problem is, our food system is broken.'"[37] Probably not something you want to say to Sarah. She offered that her response to such a statement would be, "The problem with your problem is, it's wrong."

Sarah's point is that what so many find horribly broken about the system is, in reality, the food system working exactly as it was designed and intended.

> *The problem isn't that the machine that chugs along, producing the biggest harvest the world has ever known is stalled out, that there's a broken bulb or some crossed wires. It's that the machine was built to prioritize just about one thing—cheap food. And it's working like a charm.*

Sarah is making the "it's a feature, not a bug" point about the way the food system currently operates. It reminds me of those blue jeans that already have holes in them when they are new.[38] Anyone who looks at them and thinks, "Oh my, you accidentally purchased a pair of worn-out blue jeans," just doesn't fully understand the current state of sartorial stupidity. In short, Sarah's explanation is best captured in the title of her Medium post: "The Problem With the Food System Is It Works."

By the middle of last century, the same assets that had undergirded America's contribution to the Allied Forces in WWII were deployed for agricultural production. The mainstreaming of

---

37. Sarah Mock, "The Problem with the Food System Is It Works," Medium, November 18, 2018, *https://sarah-k-mock.medium.com/the-problem-with-the-food-system-is-it-works-39604d56a84f.*

38. When I was young, holes in blue jeans were patched. One of the many reasons I fell in love with my wife in college is because we both came to learn that during the height of the Jams dungarees phenomenon, our parents refused to pay the outlandish price for the name brand version. Instead, she and I got to wear "Ma'ams"—Jams sewn from scratch by our mothers and grandmothers. The ability to discuss this trauma openly obviously led us to a deeper form of affection for each other.

manufactured pesticides and fertilizers laid the groundwork for an abundance that has confounded elected officials hoping to avoid any farm from ever going out of business ever since. The farmer population began its precipitous numeric decline along with the same trend among the rural population generally, but this was no travesty, as increasing efficiency meant that fewer and fewer farmers were needed to supply a growing domestic and international market.

In other words, our farming and food system has consistently fulfilled its mission. Producing food. Lots of it. As inexpensively and sustainably as possible given the technology and knowledge of the time.

Sarah is right. For those who call out the current state of agricultural affairs as broken, they overlook that the system has provided its customers with precisely what they wanted. Or, in some cases, what the government wanted. That said, the technology that allowed the farmers of the second half of the twentieth century to meet the demands of those days is the very same technology that many food system outsiders are questioning today. The same technology that was deployed to get vegetables to the front lines in theater has allowed us to fill the center aisles of grocery stores with food that is shelf stable for years. Forget the 1920s assurance of "a chicken for every pot." By the 1960s, Americans had hauled in the deep freezers, stacked their shelves with canned food, and witnessed an extraordinary expansion of government programs whose function was to give food away.

So is it actually broken? Does it need to be blown to smithereens so we can start over? You will have to decide for yourself. I personally do not believe that something that gives us what has been demanded of it is broken. Then again, one of the main ideas presented in these pages is that there are new players who are now asking the system for different things. Some of them are genuine. Some of them are genuinely ignorant. And some are sinister. It is in the best interests of Mercy for Animals or an alternative meat company to convince you that animal agriculture is decimating you and the planet. An agricultural law scholar in the higher education publish-or-perish regime might need to generate proposals to reform the food system that will never see the light of day inside the legislative branch of government. Or anywhere.

What is undeniable is the rising fervor among those who believe their role is to pick up the pieces and put the system back together again.[39] To do that, they have to convincingly establish that it's broken. They don't have to convince everyone. Just the right ones. My fear is they are making tremendous progress on that effort.

The food system outsiders are smart and motivated. They are equipped and well-funded. And they are busy. They believe the food system has had a great fall.

39. As best we can tell, the original Humpty Dumpty was not even an agricultural product. Certainly not an egg. Military historians tell us that Humpty Dumpty was a canon the Royalists used during the English Civil War. Ripley's Believe It or Not, "The Egg-Citing Truth Behind Humpty Dumpty," Ripley's, July 4, 2019, *https://www.ripleys.com/weird-news/humpty-dumpty/*.

CHAPTER THREE

Food Glorious Food—Which Might Explain Some Things

If you're a parent, you've been there. You hear the call in the middle of the night from your child's room down the hall, and two emotions immediately overtake your brain.

The first is one of dread: "What now? I was sleeping so good." The second is one of pride: "This will really help me when I get nominated for 'parent of the year.'" Then it is off to the rescue.

Ten minutes later, you are teetering either on the edge of triumph or defeat, still sleepy eyed, convinced by then that you should have been able to coax your child back to sleep or, in the defeat column, growing increasingly cognizant that you're in for a long haul.

I remember exactly how one of these nighttime episodes ended for me. I had, in my mind, done everything right. I had approached gingerly, with the lights still off. I allowed my daughter to explain the problem. I whispered my way through some comforting guidance. I scratched her back and rubbed her head. Her eyes blinked longer and longer and eventually closed. I stopped talking, eventually stopped touching her, and finally rose slowly off the side of the bed.

I made it all the way to the bedroom door, and just as I had barely touched the handle, I heard five soft, sweetly spoken words I will never forget: "Daddy, what's for breakfast tomorrow?"

How is it that little girls know exactly what to say to make their daddy feel so proud?

It appeared that my lifelong love of food, and events that revolve around food, had been, either genetically or by my expert teaching and mentoring, passed along to my daughter. It was also apparent that the crisis-level event that had erupted just fifteen minutes earlier was now in the rear-view mirror. I answered the question (because I'm certain I knew), and we both went back to sleep.

Like my daughter, so many of us look forward to our dates with food. What is a family gathering without the comfort food we are used to seeing there? Is it really a holiday gathering without Granny Eunice's Franklin Nut Cake? Or Grandma Pauline's fruit salad?[40] Is a college football game really a game without tailgate food? Is a wedding a wedding without a reception laden with exquisite snacks or a three-course meal? Did you really win a sports match if you didn't get to have the postgame celebratory ice cream? A movie without popcorn?[41] In almost every aspect of our lives, food is not an

40. Seriously. If you've never eaten Franklin Nut Cake, find the recipe on the internet or write me and I will send you the one I use. It requires four sticks of butter, so it has to be good. It takes about four hours to make, but it is so worth it. And the trick to my grandmother's fruit salad is the secret ingredient called sugar. Lots of it.

41. There already exists a growing body of research to prove that, during the pandemic, movie watchers did not ditch their popcorn just because fewer of them were going to movie theaters. Garrett Smith, president of American Pop Corn Company in Sioux

afterthought or an ancillary part of our agendas, gatherings, and events. It *is* the agenda.

Food is not just a part of our entertainment. In many cases, it *is* the entertainment. You would be hard pressed to scroll through the TV guide (the generic one, does the name brand one even still exist?) without seeing a myriad of cooking shows, some couched as competitions and some as restaurant rehabilitation missions. My wife's favorite part of old *Law & Order* episodes is watching the investigators eat street food or poke around with chopsticks in square takeout boxes while discussing the details of a case.

Still don't think food is our alternative love language? Wander through your favorite bookstore—in person or electronically. You will be amazed at the sheer volume (and beauty) of cookbooks available for sale. Speaking of cookbooks, much can be deduced by a stroll through the church-endorsed cookbooks of the past, complete with amazing recipes containing inordinate amounts of butter and replete with scripture to support such styles of eating. At my house, we have a saying: Butter makes it better. Amen.[42]

Should we wade into the online presence of food, food topics, and food themes? Who can resist a click-bait article ranking each state's top burger, barbecue, or pizza joint? And don't get me started

---

City, Iowa, said in an article chronicling the industry's growth that while institutional sales of popcorn tanked in 2020 because movie theaters and ballparks were closed, "sales of microwave and raw popcorn through supermarkets exploded." Ed Finkel, "State of the Industry 2020: Popcorn sales explode," *Snack Food and Wholesale Bakery,* July 17, 2020, *https://www.snackandbakery.com/articles/94976-state-of-the-industry-2020-popcorn-sales-explode.*

42. President Lincoln established the Department of Agriculture in 1862. In less than thirty-five years, it had apparently accomplished so much of its original mission that it had time to start telling Americans what to eat. This almost completely fruitless exercise continues today, although the process has been formalized over the years and now includes the added wisdom of the Department of Health and Human Services. From 1943 to 1955, USDA used a colored wheel with seven different slots to demonstrate what Americans should eat every day "to build strong bodies." Butter and fortified margarine got their own category, albeit in the seventh slots on the wheel. Last time I checked, one could still purchase one of the original posters on eBay, which concluded: "In addition to the basic 7 . . . eat any other foods you want."

on the helpful Twitter foodie world, complete with hashtags like #FoodPorn and #Foodie. And if you've never shared a picture of your plate on Facebook, then don't ask me to become your electronic friend. I'm not all that interested in the pictures of your bathroom renovation. I want to see the food!

At first, it is tempting to conclude that the strong emotions many of us have toward food are tied only to its deliciousness. After all, if something tastes good to us, we generally crave it or want more of it. An opposite point of view is apparently held by some who view food merely as a source of calories. I don't know any of those people. And I'm not sure I want to.

But over the years, researchers and cultural observers have made more sweeping observations about our connection to food. Mary C. Henderson, of what was Paterson State College and is now William Paterson University of New Jersey, postulates that the role of food in society has been underappreciated through the years: "The study of food has undergone a curious, varied, and altogether unsatisfactory and incomplete analysis as a prime factor in the development of people and cultures."[43]

Henderson is onto something. Food is culture. There are few major events, much less holidays, in which remembrances of the event itself do not also include remembrances of the food eaten there.

Food often helps us know—or at least feel like we know—other people. I recently read a beautiful obituary for my boss's father. It recounted his service in the U.S. Navy, ticked off a list of sons, grandkids, and extended family, and mentioned his career path and engagement with his church and social clubs. But the part I remember most was the mention of "spiedies" (SPEE-dees), sandwiches

43. Mary C. Henderson, "Food as communication in American culture," *Today's Speech* 18, (1970), 3-8.

rarely served outside of his native New York, but which I now feel compelled to find and try.[44]

It is not out of the ordinary that an obituary would mention a favorite food, whether it's one the deceased had consumed regularly or perhaps one they used to prepare. I would like for my obituary to include lavish praise for my amazing Beef Wellington. Now, to be clear, I don't make amazing Beef Wellington, or for that matter even average, or any, Beef Wellington, but I wish I did. And I wish I did it so well it showed up in my death records.

What does that tell us? Surely it signals that connections to food go far beyond taste and calories. In his excellent book *Alchemy*, Rory Sutherland recalls the food futurists of the last century opining that we would, by now, receive our nutrition mostly through pills and supplements that allowed us to skip eating meals altogether.[45] Sutherland appropriately points out the stupidity of this idea, which was based on the wildly mistaken belief that we eat food for its nutritive value.

A collection of essays pulled together by a group of students at the University of Kansas entitled *The Role of Food in American Society* contains the following observation:

> *[T]hroughout history, the sharing of food has served as the lubricant to produce an atmosphere of camaraderie and congeniality. As anthropologists and historians have emphasized, religious rituals, holidays and festivals emphasize food's power to bind individuals into communities and symbolize their unity and goodwill toward one another.*[46]

44. Good for me there's a Spiedie Turtle right here in Raleigh, NC—a green food truck that serves these scrumptious marinated meat subs.

45. Rory Sutherland, *Alchemy* (n.p.: Morrow, 2019), 51.

46. Hannah Ballard et al., *The Role of Food in American Society*, University of Kansas, n.d. Available at: *https://kuscholarworks.ku.edu/bitstream/handle/1808/6329/The%20Role%20of%20Food.pdf?sequence=1.*

Indeed. Thank God for lubricants to camaraderie and congeniality. I can stand almost any obnoxious party guest if the food is good enough. And if there is enough of it.

Ask a diplomat about lubricants to camaraderie. They may mention alcohol. But chances are they will also point out that, at the highest levels of government, food is a key part of diplomacy.

I remember traveling to China with the North Carolina Commissioner of Agriculture, Steve Troxler, back in 2009. I also remember being grateful that I was not the guest of honor—which meant I didn't have to eat like the guest of honor, consistently sampling things that I had never seen served as food in my native Sampson County, North Carolina. And I've seen a lot of things served as food in my native Sampson County.[47]

Do not move past the Jayhawks' summation (above) too quickly. Not only is food useful to loosen folks up, it can also bring them together. Note the reference to the ability of food to "bind individuals into communities." Perhaps if you've ever learned that a stranger and you share a "favorite" restaurant in a faraway place, you've seen this phenomenon at work. We all recollect the food from our elementary school (rectangular pizza, always served with corn?), the doughnuts at that one particular shop down on the boardwalk (like Britt's at Carolina Beach or Sherry's Bakery in Dunn), or that hot dog from the hole-in-the-wall place. Food and our culinary experiences bind us to one another and are natural extensions of our sense of place.

---

47. I also remember being excited to visit with the founder of a bread museum in Serbia when I was a German Marshall Fund Fellow. I had read that he wanted to start a museum about bread because some form of bread could be found in all cultures for at least the last two thousand years. I am not even sure he was right about that. Regardless, our meeting turned out to have very little substance, as he served homemade vodka in the first five minutes of our delegation's arrival and everything after that is a little hazy. By the way, drink is food, at least according to Congress: "The term 'food' means (1) articles used for food or drink for man or other animals, (2) chewing gum, and (3) articles used for components of any such article." 21 U.S.C. sec. 321. Most foods are probably jealous that gum got its own callout.

One more quote. This one from Amy S. Choi, although I'm sure others have said it, too: "Food feeds the soul."[48]

Ever heard of soul food? Comfort food? Once we stop to think about it, it is abundantly clear that for most of us, the value of food is not just in its nutrition. In fact, sometimes the value has nothing to do with feeding our bodies in a literal sense. Sometimes, food is valuable *solely* because of the psychological impact it has within our minds and hearts. One personal observation of mine, and others, is that at least part of our obesity epidemic is a result of folks attempting to fill a hole in their hearts or minds by putting something in their mouths. Worthy of much more extrapolation than space provides here, I personally know the futility of attempting to fill Pascal's God-shaped hole in our hearts with things we put in our stomachs. But growing up as a Southern Baptist, I was taught that it was okay to try! Molly Zemek, who for most of her adult life has been known for her extraordinary culinary skills, honed while receiving her Grande Diplome from Le Cordon Bleu (the one in Paris, not the one in the freezer section at Costco), is now known for her weight-management coaching skills. She writes: "Food was not the problem; my thoughts were."[49] Note the point: in our age of abundance, we have become wired to reach for food with anticipation that it will fill not just our stomachs, but our hearts and minds, too.

At first, I thought of the term "foodie" as describing only the most elite eater. Only those who can identify the cut of meat without the label or tell you what is in a dish just by tasting it. The gastronomes and gourmets who think of food the way a woodworker thinks of a piece of burl ash. To them, cooking or eating are adventures, and

48. Amy Choi, "What Americans Can Learn From Other Food Cultures," *Ideas.Ted.Com*, December 18, 2014, *https://ideas.ted.com/what-americans-can-learn-from-other-food-cultures/*.

49. "Molly Zemek Coaching," About, Molly Zemek, last modified 2021, *https://www.mollyzemek.com/about*.

finding or re-creating the beauty and satisfaction of food is personally rewarding.

For the purposes of this book, the definition is broader. And indeed, the crowd-sourced arbiter of definitions Wikipedia has at one time or another defined a foodie as one who "seeks new food experiences as a hobby rather than simply eating out of convenience or hunger."[50] That likely describes all of us on one day or another. And that's the point. We are surrounded by foodies.

Remember the quote from Secretary Perdue? "When man has no food, he has one problem, when man has plenty of food, he has plenty of problems." Foodies—those who make food purchasing and consumption decisions for reasons beyond convenience and hunger—are consistently finding new problems. Indeed in many cases, they have found problems within the very system that has provided them with such an affordable, abundant food supply for decades.

In the late 1990s, I was a part of a program sponsored by my home state's largest land grant institution. It was called "Food . . . for Thought." The idea behind the program was to engage the University in the task of reminding people across the state where their food comes from. It was targeted at urbanites and mainly at the thought leaders in our state's largest population centers. We had a road show that included a pop-up booth and artwork adorned with stats and figures, a table that held glossy handouts and refrigerator magnets, and a recent graduate of the College of Agriculture and Life Sciences who presented a thrilling speech that included memorable lines like "food doesn't come just from the grocery store." (You guessed it. I was that recent graduate.)

If you had asked those of us involved in the campaign what success would have looked like, we would have told you that we wanted people to think more about their food, and to think about

---

50. "Foodies," Article, Wikipedia, last modified July 28, 2021, *https://en.wikipedia.org/wiki/Foodie*.

it all the way back to its source. The hope was that such reflection would help people understand the complexity of the food system, the efficiency of the American farmer, and the miracle it is that we have access to fully stocked grocery aisles day in and day out.

We must have been wildly successful. Or perhaps we had good timing. Thinking about where food comes from is now the hip thing to do.

In 1995, which was before our "Food . . . for Thought" campaign, David Marshall edited *Food Choice and the Consumer* with an eye toward further exploring exactly why most Americans "like what they eat" instead of "eat what they like." Marshall's work documents what was likely the beginning of the foodie movement. At the time of his book, issues like taste, convenience, and affordability all seemed to be the predominant drivers of food choice. Concerns about animal welfare show up on the list, but at that time they warranted only a "trend to watch" kind of mention.

In fact, the book quotes a report prepared for the US Food Marketing Institute by Faith Popcorn. That is not a joke. You are welcome to think Faith's name is unique, just don't ignore her findings. *Fortune* magazine has named her the "Nostradamus of Marketing," and she is a renowned American trend expert.[51]

Popcorn identified ten major trends in consumer attitudes and their likely impact on food choice. Looking back now with the benefit of hindsight, it is clear she nailed it. At the beginning of the list were things like a desire for better quality produce with minimal processing, and a prediction that demand for single-serve portions and ready-to-eat meals would grow in the coming years. But at the very end was a prediction that was absolute clairvoyance.

Coming in at number ten on the list was Popcorn's prediction of "a declining narcissism and a search for moral stability in food choice decisions."

51. "Faith Popcorn," Faith Popcorn, Faith Popcorn's Brain Reserve, last modified June 22, 2020, *https://faithpopcorn.com/faith-popcorn/*.

I'm not so sure about the declining narcissism. You can draw your own conclusions about that. But the search for "moral stability," or ethics in food choice, is undoubtedly spot on.

Here's a quote from John Ikerd, a retired agricultural economist with six books to his name, along with recognition as a leader in the loosely defined agricultural sustainability movement. In an essay entitled "The New American Food Culture," he writes: "Eating is a moral act . . . Although we may not give it much thought, what we choose to eat is a reflection of our basic values and beliefs."[52]

And Bob Martin, director of Food System Policy, Johns Hopkins Center for a Livable Future, has said, "I do think food is kind of *the* social issue of our time."

Ethics? Basic values and beliefs? *The* social issue of our time?

Perhaps we've taken the advice of not discussing religion and politics among acquaintances, and food has become the religion and politics of our age. Recall the previous chapter, where we covered the widespread critique that our food system is broken. Why do you think so many people believe that when they hear it?[53] In fact, why are people thinking about it at all? Why are so many so committed to their beliefs that food needs fixing? Particularly when the agriculture community felt so invisible and underappreciated just two decades ago that they started campaigns to beg folks to think more about where their food comes from?

There are likely multiple reasons. Here are just three I find most convincing, in order of increasing complexity. First, as established above, while food is special to all of us, it is also something we

52. John Ikerd, "The New American Food Culture," University of Missouri, n.d., *https://web.missouri.edu/~ikerdj/papers/SFTFoodCulture.htm*.

53. If I have asked one person that question, I have asked one thousand. What I'm searching out is the "why" beyond the "what." We know they believe the food system needs to be rewired, but even if we assume for the sake of argument that is true, what motivates them to elevate that concern over so many other vexing ills in our society?

interact with every single day.[54] Generally multiple times in a day. For me, almost hourly. Most of us choose from dozens of restaurants, hundreds of menu items, and tens of thousands of products on the shelves of our grocery stores multiple times a week. To us, food is known, and we are accustomed to having it our way. It is ubiquitous in our lives, our homes, and our culture.

That almost constant interaction creates a riper atmosphere for pondering the complexities of the food system. Consider that you may only pump gas once a week, only see stories about dire consequences in foreign lands occasionally, or do not really appreciate the volume of goods moved on trains unless you're waiting for the track to clear.

That it is so close and so frequently within our reach leads then to the easy conclusion that it is something each of us can—and in fact should be able to—control.

In the words of Marshall Stewart, Chief Engagement Officer for the University of Missouri System, "Agriculture is in many ways a victim of its success. With food quality, safety, variety and prices being so reasonable, the consumer has taken it for granted and therefore emotions and feelings become drivers of policy at the expense of science." We believe we can demand more from the incredible food system that we already have without really sacrificing much from ourselves. The trade-offs for what most consumers believe would be an improved food system seem, therefore, to be extraordinarily low.

The second explanation for this evolution of thought builds on the first. If the first part is true, then with very little cost to themselves, consumers feel when they make certain purchases that they will have done something better for their children, their community, or their planet. In a nutshell, of all the problems we cannot fix as individuals because of their complexity—pandemics, global

54. Unless you're like the otherwise nice lady in my office who fasts for thirty-six hours at a time. I do not advise asking her questions in expectation of a cheery response in those last ten to twelve hours.

warming, conflict in the Middle East—we think food is one we can. It is precisely because we are so close to it that we believe we can demand that it give us more. Too busy to volunteer at the local shelter? Too tired to help with homework? Maybe—but let me put this sustainable product in my online shopping bag. Sign me up to save the food system. After all, I read somewhere that it can be done in three easy steps. And make no mistake—there's a label or marketing scheme ready to capitalize on any consumer's desire to do just that. The famous "eat this, not that" cliché comes to mind.

Third, and consistent with the title of this chapter, in our culture, the food we choose, and the opinions we have about how it was stewarded and served, has become just one more form of identity.

I've been consistently inspired by the teachings of Dr. Tim Keller, a Presbyterian minister, author whose books have sold millions of copies, and extraordinarily capable Christian apologist and theologian. He has given hundreds of sermons, dozens of "talks" and keynotes, and numerous interviews. While there are many themes to his work, his most attractive to me is his recognition of modern society's struggle with true identity.[55] Within those teachings, he observes that so much of today's psychological unease is a result of so many individuals attempting to perform their way into a specific identity.

I believe that some of what we see in the foodie movement and its attendant food system Humpty Dumptyism is an expression of that search for identity. At very little social cost, and for almost no personal cost, most women and men in modern-day American society can reach for the label that has just the right words to make them feel a little better about their purchase.[56] There is an affirmation that comes from shopping amongst the most hip, the most progressive,

55. This sentence is not meant to suggest that Dr. Keller preaches anything other than the Good News. In my view, however, he brings his readers and listeners to an understanding of that Good News in ways that speak directly to our modern day society's seemingly recurring cycle of exhaustion and frustration.

56. Note that I say "most." There remain many who have to choose between $1.29 a pound and $0.99 a pound. One of the enduring frustrations of the outsider-in farming and

and the most affluent grocery store customers of our day. When doing so, we see ourselves as them. We take on the identity of the responsible consumer and, by extension, responsible citizen.

All of us, your author included, are subject to the allure of the psychological boost that comes from thinking we are what we eat and where we shop. If the label—or a podcast or blog article—says it's better for me, my fellow man, or the environment, then I am obviously a better person if I make the choice to purchase that more socially responsible product. I can now proudly wear the mantle of being a foodie—or even a "good foodie," which you will read about in the next few pages. The psychological boost from this form of retail therapy is much more satisfying than what can be gained from buying plain ole meat and potatoes. Food choices and personal views of food and farming are a form of self-identification and self-expression. Defying "big food" and "big agriculture" is a form of resistance, which again, feeds our own self-worth and the perception of our own identities.

None of this should be read as suggesting that critics of the modern farming and food systems are mean, completely wrong, unintelligent, or weird. The point is, however, that there is often some sanctimony associated with the modern-day foodie's views of the system, and that observation frankly should not be surprising.

Turns out it is not just my daughter and I who think about our next meal several hours before it is due. I suppose the miniscule efforts of my early twenties to get urbanites to think more about where their food comes from have come full circle. Food, glorious food, indeed. In a country as blessed as ours, it's a new religion.

So what are the most recent creeds and testaments of this new religion? To the extent that outsiders are successfully influencing consumers, what does that look like? Read on and find out.

---

food-reform movement is that it promotes ideas that will undoubtedly increase price pressure on the most economically marginalized in our communities.

CHAPTER FOUR

THE FOODIE OF THE FUTURE AND WHY FARMERS SHOULD CARE

In the now decades-old romantic comedy film *What Women Want*, Mel Gibson played the role of an advertising executive who miraculously developed the ability to telepathically understand what women were thinking. Not a bad skill for a marketing executive to develop.[57]

At first, he was surprised to learn that women did not have the same admiration for him as he did for himself. In the end, Gibson used his newfound skill for self-reflection and changed his persona.

57. Or a husband, for that matter. I once heard a newly minted husband say, while pointing to his wife, "She didn't come with an owners manual." (They are still married, some twenty-one years later. He must've found a helpful YouTube video.)

He dramatically improved his standing with the women in his life, and with one woman in particular: his daughter.

There is a lesson here for agriculture. If farmers and agribusiness players want to understand the future of food, they must consistently try to better understand the people who are going to buy it. And those people are complicated. Unfortunately, we do not yet have any movies about farmers who have developed the Mel Gibson-like talent of hearing what consumers are thinking as they rove the grocery aisles—physically or online. But if we did, I bet they would be hilarious. Until then, farmers and their food value chain brethren must study market research to try to understand the preferences of consumers and what on earth is driving their (sometimes inexplicable) purchasing decisions.

Despite what the experts tell us, there is no way to fully divine the state of mind of the modern-day consumer. More importantly, there are some inconsistencies that simply cannot be reconciled. For example, the research reveals that we are entering a more "health conscious" shopping and eating era. Yet every time I go to a local fried chicken restaurant, the line to place an order is wrapped around the block. And trust me, I perform this experiment often. Just to further the research, of course.

On a similar note, the data shared below will suggest that convenience is a major factor in food selection. At the same time, we all know people who drive well out of their way, sometimes to a completely different part of town, for a certain ice cream, meat product, or doughnut.[58] So, today's consumer is for convenience, except when they aren't. Another observation that often leaves farmers shaking their heads is that the research reveals that consumers are reaching for food packages that contain certain buzzwords. Clean, or

58. For me it is liver mush. Ironically, the pork liver mush quality in my home state is better the farther one drives from the most dominant pork producing parts of the state. Speaking of liver mush, I once wrote a three-page legal memo on the differences between liver mush and liver pudding. Astonishingly, the firm where I performed this critical summer associate task still offered me a job.

true, or simple, for example. Still other research makes clear that those consumers often have mistaken ideas about what those words mean—legally or even practically.

In short, how are those of us in the agriculture and food ministry supposed to minister to the lost foodie souls wandering around if even *they* do not really know what they want? Well, admittedly, everything we see forecasted will not come true. But some of it will. And more striking than the inconsistencies and the missed predictions is the risk of not continually searching for where consumers are going and attempting to align our industry with their preferences. Chances are that if we don't, someone else will.

To be fair, those of us engaged in discussions about farming and agriculture are already pretty good at this consumer research analysis thing. It would be difficult to attend any commodity association's national meeting without hearing from at least one speaker whose task is to educate farmers and other ag insiders on the latest consumer trends. Such presenters typically offer some predictions on what products will do well in the consumer market in the coming months and years.

The National Pork Board hosted one such discussion that I was fortunate enough to attend in mid-2021. Dr. Shelley Balanko, senior vice president at the Hartman Group, offered a presentation entitled "Consumer and Food Culture Trends for Tomorrow's Strategies." Dr. Balanko is an applied psychologist in every sense of the word, putting her training to work in deciphering consumer behavior for her clients, mostly in the food space. The Hartman Group, out of Bellevue, Washington, has studied American food and beverage culture for years, using thorough methodologies that allow them to paint a picture of where we are going. You will see me refer to Hartman and its significant body of research multiple times in the coming pages.

FROM GOOD FOOD TO GOOD FOODIE

Dr. Balanko's presentation was, as these sorts of talks usually are, a treasure trove of insight. Most memorable was her introduction of the term "good foodie."[59] She defined the "good foodie" as a person "with a passion for food *and who eats with empathy*." This evolution of the foodie from a person who possesses a discernment for food and taste to a person who cares about food and taste *and its entire life cycle* is consistent with the points made in the previous chapter. As we have established, food is—almost anywhere in the world—more than a way to meet caloric intake. As such, the only question we might have about this good foodie trend is why it didn't happen sooner.

More importantly, Balanko identified the good foodie as an early adopter. A market leader. This indicates that such a person would likely be a trend-setter and that this view of eating would spread. The overall takeaway was that if you thought the modern-day foodie was discerning, wait until you meet tomorrow's *good* foodie.

The industry often refers to this new value paradigm as manifesting "consumer consciousness." The headline of an October 1, 2019, *New York Times* article reads "How to Be a More Conscious Consumer, Even If You're on a Budget," but the real story was buried in the byline: "Most of us financially support companies we might not necessarily support socially, ethically, or philosophically."[60]

---

59. For some reason, adding "good" to the term "foodie" seems repetitively redundant. It reminds me of the Ray Stevens song "Jeremiah Peabody's Polyunsaturated, Quick Dissolving, Fast Acting, Pleasant Tasting, Green and Purple Pills." The refrain reads: "Get ridda that runny nose, that nagging cough, that sneeze, achoo, that wheeze and other injuries. Take the wonder drug that cures all your ills, take Jeremiah Peabody's polyunsaturated, quick dissolving, fast acting, pleasant tasting green and purple pills." Ray Stevens Music, "Ray Stevens - Jeremiah Peabody's Polyunsaturated Quick-Dissolving . . . Green & Purple Pills," YouTube video, 0:46, posted July 15, 2009, *https://www.youtube.com/watch?v=jQIfp1TAo2I*. Then again, hold that food as the wonder drug that cures all your ills thought. It's coming.

60. Kristin Wong, "How to Be a More Conscious Consumer, Even If You're on a Budget," *The New York Times*, updated November 6, 2019, *https://www.nytimes.com/2019/10/01/smarter-living/sustainabile-shopping-conscious-consumer.html*.

That is a damning characterization. It is nonetheless likely an accurate one. But that is apparently going to change.

Now more than ever, maxims like "conscious consumption," "people, planet, profit," and "fair food" are capturing the attention of food buyers in the United States and around the world. Perhaps it is easier to shift to "conscious" consumption than to just cut back on consumption altogether. After all, we feel a little less guilty eating that "sustainable" decadent chocolate or popping those doughnuts out of an eco-friendly clamshell before we stuff them in our faces. And we agree, don't we, that it is easier to justify eating ice cream purchased right at the dairy than the same product bought at a grocery store? I have always thought the flies around the nearby herd were distracting and would therefore prefer to get mine to go. Here again, it is not really about the calories and nutrition (yet) as much as it is about the story.

Nestlé Professional, the world's largest food and beverage company,[61] partners with foodservice providers—their customers—to continually ensure that their food offerings reflect the latest shifts in consumer preferences. In 2020, Nestlé noted that a top trend was "sustainability, transparency, and ethical sourcing."[62]

Nestlé's observations correlate closely with those made by Emma Weston, the CEO and co-founder of AgriDigital, a company bridging the gap between farmers and consumers by making grain supply chains more traceable. According to Weston:

> *One of the top trends driving agriculture . . . is around provenance and supply chain traceability.*

61. "Our Company," About Us, Nestlé, last modified September 5, 2014, *https://www.nestleprofessional.us/section/our-company.*

62. "Food and Beverage Industry Trends 2020," Consumer Intelligence, Nestlé, last modified February 6, 2020, *https://www.nestleprofessional.us/trend-reports/food-and-beverage-industry-trends-2020?gclid=CjwKCAiA8Jf-BRB-EiwAWDtEGvBshAqBz7u83t-qJdweQ3lmyHY_gEaS0hV3WyVlKPi-na0rZfCArBoCRSgQAvD_BwE.*

> *Consumers are demanding greater transparency about where their food comes from and how it is produced and are seeking out producers who are using technologies such as blockchain, IoT and smart labelling to provide this level of detail.*[63]

Just two decades ago, the most oft-repeated frustration at agricultural commodity association meetings was that consumers take farmers for granted, almost always showing no interest in where their food comes from beyond the grocery store. The farmers hoped this would change over time, and even sponsored campaigns to remind consumers that food doesn't come just from the grocery store. As mentioned in Chapter 3, I was a proud participant in some of these efforts, speaking to business executives in multiple cities, frequently circling back to the farm organizations to tell them our efforts were working.[64]

Be careful what you wish for.

Fast forward to today and consumers are focusing more and more on how their food is grown, transported, processed, and packaged. NPD Group food industry analyst Darren Seifer observes: "More and more consumers are concerned with how products they purchase came to market. The story of the company has become a much larger part of the decision-making process for consumers than it [was] in the past."[65]

This particular shift seems to have two key drivers. The first is a generational one, with Millennials and Generation Z focusing more

---

63. Sam Mire, "What Trends Are Shaping Agriculture in 2019? 13 Experts Share Their Insights," *Disruptor Daily,* June 29, 2019, *https://www.disruptordaily.com/agriculture-trends/.*

64. I still have one of the refrigerator magnets we gave away, complete with the "Food . . . for Thought" logo emblazoned across it.

65. Audrey Altmann, "Understanding what today's eco-conscious food consumers want," *SmartBrief,* September 9, 2020, *https://www.smartbrief.com/original/2020/09/understanding-what-today%E2%80%99s-eco-conscious-food-consumers-want.*

on environmental ethics and sustainability than the generations that came before them.

The second driver is one that I believe can be traced back to the efficiency and capabilities of American farmers. Namely, most consumers in the United States are in a position to demand more. Remember that when mankind has plenty to eat, he has many problems? Societies with grave food insecurity probably don't tweet the latest Kardashian food craze or ask how many square feet an animal had at its disposal while gestating.

Our consumers have the means and the access to make discerning choices not just about the taste and appearance of food itself but also about how it was raised, processed, and brought to market. Simply put, our consumers can afford to be more discerning. Food purchasers in the United States spend a lower percentage of their disposable income on food than purchasers in any other country in the world.[66] It is from that vantage point, which indeed should be celebrated and not disdained, that average grocery store guests can become picky foodies, contemplating extras like food miles or that shiitake mushroom's carbon footprint.

In the remainder of this chapter, we will take a closer look at the demographics of the most influential consumers. In the next one, we will look more sharply at the trends they are driving.

WHO DRIVES THE SHOPPING CART?

Sales professionals will tell you it is important to be friendly to everyone, but they really want to get to the decision maker. In the food world, the classic definitions of the customer are changing.

Conventional wisdom suggests the woman is still the Chief Purchasing Officer in each home, but that trend could be shifting.

---

66. Alex Gray, "Which countries spend the most on food? This map will show you," *World Economic Forum,* December 7, 2016, *https://www.weforum.org/agenda/2016/12/this-map-shows-how-much-each-country-spends-on-food/*.

As recently as late 2019, the Pew Research Center published an analysis of Bureau of Labor Statistics data that found that women typically dominate food preparation and grocery shopping in the United States. Among married or cohabiting parents with children, mothers prepare the meals or are the primary grocery shopper 80 percent of the time.[67] A slightly smaller group, 71 percent, say they primarily handle both the shopping and the meal prep, including cleanup. While the shopping and preparation time is shorter for families or households without children, women still spend approximately twice as much time as men on these tasks.[68] Assuming we can trust the bean counters in government, this should be pretty reliable data. That does not mean, however, that there isn't conflicting data that suggest it is the men who are literally bringing home the bacon.

In fact, in 2017, respondents in a *Men's Health* survey reported that a much higher percentage of men, some 84 percent, are the primary shopper and food prepper.[69] Of course, this survey polled only men, presumably without their significant others or roommates peering over their shoulders.[70] It seems impossible to square this

---

67. Katherine Schaeffer, "Among U.S. Couples, Women Do More Cooking and Grocery Shopping Than Men," *Pew Research Center*, September 24, 2019, *https://www.pewresearch.org/fact-tank/2019/09/24/among-u-s-couples-women-do-more-cooking-and-grocery-shopping-than-men/*.

68. It is important to note that the BLS data at issue in this particular analysis is based on time tracking diaries produced by the respondents in the study. The American Time Use Survey has been conducted by the U.S. Census Bureau since 2003, and this particular data is drawn from the Eating and Health Module.

69. Abha Bhattarai, "Grocery Stores Are Adapting to More Male Shoppers—Whom They Treat Like Knuckleheads," *The Washington Post*, July 27, 2017, *https://www.washingtonpost.com/news/business/wp/2017/07/27/grocery-stores-are-adapting-to-more-male-shoppers-who-they-treat-like-knuckleheads/*.

70. Additionally, the *Men's Health* survey does not appear to have been focused solely on actively parenting households. A single man, living alone, is most likely the primary shopper and food prepper for his household. Go figure. Notably, the *Men's Health* survey was conducted completely online, another red flag for those accustomed to regularly evaluating polling data, unless very careful precautions are followed.

data with that produced by the Bureau of Labor Statistics, but it doesn't make sense to completely discount it either.

Maybe there is no clear gender winner of the dominant shopper title.

Recall Dr. Balanko, mentioned earlier? Her employer, the Hartman Group, is frequently tapped by the Food Marketing Institute (FMI) and other key food industry players to gather insights that guide the industry in understanding customer behavior and shopping habits. Hartman retains anthropologists, social scientists, and business analysts who have studied American food and beverage culture for over thirty years. They report that while grocery shopping is increasingly a shared task, women are still more likely to be the "main shopper."[71] But to be clear, that doesn't mean they are the only shopper. In fact, as explored below, men may actually make more trips to the store, and other data suggest that men's food shopping status is clearly climbing.

Winsight, LLC describes itself as a B2B (business to business) information services company that focuses on the food and beverage industry, providing insight and market intelligence for business leaders in every channel where consumers buy food and beverages.[72] They accomplish this by continually researching industry trends, convening food and beverage industry stakeholders, and publishing information those stakeholders find relevant as they try to navigate the discerning—and sometimes not so discerning—American consumer.

According to Denver-based Jennifer Strailey, who also happens to be the editor in chief of Winsight's Grocery Business publication, men's total grocery spend is about the same as women's. She is quick

71. Hartman Group, "8 Key Takeaways From Hartman's 2018 ACT Food & Beverage Culture Summits," *Hartman Group,* December 18, 2018, *https://www.hartman-group.com/newsletters/1510692974/8-key-takeaways-from-hartmans-2018-act-food-beverage-culture-summits.*

72. "The Winsight Advantage," About, Winsight, last modified August 2019, *https://www.winsightmedia.com/about.*

to point out, however, that men shop and spend in different ways. Strailey provides the following insights about men as food shoppers:

> *He is driven by convenience and will pay a premium for it. While he shops across multiple channels, he is more likely to go to the grocery store for food. Technology is his friend, and he appreciates online ordering and mobile pay. He also shops for groceries as many times per month as his female counterparts . . . Market research data from leading industry experts . . . indicate that while their purchase patterns may be somewhat different, men's total grocery spend is about the same as women's.*

One question left unexamined here is which adult in the house really *should* do the shopping. And I'm not touching that one with a ten-foot pole.

GENERATIONAL SHIFTS

The second major dynamic to consider when tracking who drives the shopping cart is the common generational divides that economists and sociologists have studied for years.

In 2017, USDA's Economic Research Service released a 57-page deep dive examination of the food purchasing decisions of Millennials, generally comparing their food purchasing habits against other generational cohorts in the United States.[73] Using Millennials as the lodestar and then comparing other age groups to them might seem slightly offensive to those of us who do not fall

73. Annemarie Kuhns and Michelle Saksena, *Food Purchase Decisions of Millennial Households Compared to Other Generations* (United States Department of Agriculture, 2017), Economic Information Bulletin Number 186. *https://www.ers.usda.gov/webdocs/publications/86401/eib-186.pdf*

within that generational description, but it is generally where most market research begins. After all, Millennials (for our purposes, those born between 1981 and 1996) have surpassed Baby Boomers as the nation's largest living population block.

According to Pew, relying on U.S. Census data, "As of July 1, 2019, Millennials . . . numbered 72.1 million, and Boomers [born 1946–1964] numbered 71.6 million. Generation X [born 1965–1980] numbered 65.2 million and is projected to pass the Boomers in population by 2028."[74] Moreover, they are spilling out into the working world in vast numbers and have now become the largest generation in the labor force.[75] As their incomes increase, they are beginning their ascent into their greatest consuming years.

Perhaps most importantly, Millennials believe in the power of their purchases. Hartman Group CEO Laurie Demeritt has observed that "Millennials feel like they really are enacting social change by how they spend their dollars, and that makes them feel good."[76] In the words of Deloitte's Global 2021 Millennial and Gen Z Survey, they believe they can "urge accountability."[77]

So about that quintessential Millennial: according to the ERS, "Millennials place more importance on convenience and experiential attributes. For example, Millennials shop more frequently at gas stations; use same-day delivery services; and are more likely to buy organic food, hot sauce, energy drinks, and artisanal alcohol

74. Richard Fry, "Millennials overtake Baby Boomers as America's largest generation," *Pew Research Center*, April 28, 2020, *https://www.pewresearch.org/fact-tank/2020/04/28/millennials-overtake-baby-boomers-as-americas-largest-generation/*.

75. Richard Fry, "Millennials are the largest generation in the U.S. labor force," *Pew Research Center*, April 11, 2018, *https://www.pewresearch.org/fact-tank/2018/04/11/millennials-largest-generation-us-labor-force/*.

76. Elaine Watson, "What makes Millennials tick?," *FOODnavigator-usa.com*, May 26, 2016, *https://www.foodnavigator-usa.com/Article/2016/05/27/Hartman-Group-MSL-Group-talk-Millennials-and-food*.

77. Deloitte, "A Call for Accountability and Action," the Deloitte Global 2021 Millennial and Gen Z Survey. *https://www2.deloitte.com/content/dam/Deloitte/global/Documents/2021-deloitte-global-millennial-survey-report.pdf*.

beverages (Tuttle, 2015)."[78,79] Turns out there is a reason convenience stores aren't going away, even if the gas pumps do. In fact, NACS, the global trade association for convenience stores, reports that there are more than 1 million convenience stores around the world, with 152,720 in the United States.[80] In a single day in the United States, some 165 million transactions take place within a convenience store somewhere, with annual sales from such transactions just shy of $650 billion. Most of those transactions involve a food purchase.

The USDA ERS study also makes clear that Millennials purchase less food for consumption at home, and such purchases reflect a higher proportion of ready-to-eat foods than other generational groups. The data also suggest that this age group has a preference for eating out at restaurants, fast food places, and other venues outside the home.[81] One of the more humorous qualifications provided in this particular government report was that the food purchasing patterns of Millennials are somewhat obscured by the

78. Did you catch that line about hot sauce? This fits into a global trend of increased use of sauces and condiments overall, but particularly among Millennials. The *Wall Street Journal* documented this trend again in 2019 with an article titled "Hot Trend: Spicy Sauces Are on Fire," Micah Maidenberg, The *Wall Street Journal,* June 7, 2019, *https://www.wsj.com/articles/hot-trend-spicy-sauces-are-on-fire-11559899801*.

79. For many years, I presumed that the roller dogs I saw inside gas stations were the same hot dogs that had been there for ages. It was not until I commuted for six months from Raleigh to Washington, D.C., spending countless hours on Interstate 95 and the truck stops that thankfully dot this landscape, that I came to realize just how much joy can be experienced when sampling the refined, elegant taste of a roller dog, and to respect even more those filled with cheese or jalapenos. Who knew I was so hip, engaging in an experience with such "experiential attributes"? I will not elaborate on what those attributes frequently turned out to be, except to say they made my overall commute slower and some subparts much faster.

80. "About NACS," About, NACS, last modified n.d., *https://www.convenience.org/About-NACS*.

81. Annemarie Kuhns and Michelle Saksena, "Millennials Devote Larger Shares of Their Grocery Spending to Prepared Foods, Pasta, and Sugar and Sweets Than Other Generations," *USDA Economic Research Service,* December 29, 2017, *https://www.ers.usda.gov/amber-waves/2017/December/millennials-devote-larger-shares-of-their-grocery-spending-to-prepared-foods-pasta-and-sugar-and-sweets-than-other-generations/*.

fact that a significant number of them "might still live with their parents, who are the primary shoppers." (Their words, not mine.)

Millennials also prefer products that offer perceived health benefits. Reduced caffeine. Gluten free. Portion control. And they prefer fresh ingredients. Brett Sciotto, a former military intelligence officer who is now the CEO of Aimpoint Research, has explained that Millennials appear to be reversing a trend set in motion following WWII.[82] The war effort and exodus of folks off the farm that followed led to the presence of more and more processed foods on grocery shelves. Sciotto states that 61 percent of our dietary calories come from processed food, although the number is likely even higher among younger eaters.[83] Retailers are well aware of this trend, which is precisely why the number of fresh products that populate the perimeter of our grocery stores are expanding, while the rows and rows of shelf-stable ingredients in the middle appear to be shrinking.[84]

---

82. Agri-Pulse Communications, Inc., "Food and Ag Summit West: Brett Sciotto, Aimpoint," YouTube video, posted September 27, 2020, *https://www.youtube.com/watch?v=vIbOb3ebZGc&t=3170s*.

83. Lu Wang et al., "Trends in Consumption of Ultraprocessed Foods Among US Youths Aged 2-19 Years, 1999-2018," *JAMA Network,* August 10, 2021, *https://jamanetwork.com/journals/jama/article-abstract/2782866?guestAccessKey=c646e502-898f-443b-8558-d90a74e35415&utm_source=For_The_Media&utm_medium=referral&utm_campaign=ftm_links&utm_content=tfl&utm_term=081021*.

84. This is as good a place as any to point out that I absolutely love grocery shopping. I grew up in what would undoubtedly be called a food desert today. That being said, I do not know much about deserts. I do know that the two largest are in areas where it is really cold and camels do not go. But USDA obviously doesn't know much about deserts either. Their definition of a food desert is an area within a census tract in which at least five hundred people or 33 percent of the population live more than *one mile* from a supermarket or large grocery store. To their credit, they also said that for rural census tracts, this distance should be expanded to ten miles. Whereas I grew up at least twenty miles from the nearest full-service grocery store, I suppose I was in a food tundra. Or food Siberia. My mother only shopped for groceries every couple of weeks, but when she did, my brothers and I were expected to report to the back steps to tote in what I recollect to be dozens and dozens of paper sacks full of the loot. It was glorious. To this day, my wife has to choose between going to the grocery store herself, a task she hates, or letting me go, which always turns into a lengthy adventure.

Consistent with Demeritt's observation regarding Millennials' emergence as conscious consumers, the National Peanut Board, headquartered in Atlanta, points out that Millennials' purchasing decisions go "well beyond price." They include sourcing of inputs, "product inspiration, responsibility and authenticity."[85] This means they are likely driving much of the broader population's pivot to conscious consumerism.

According to a Dairy Farmers of America publication, Millennials also enjoy adventure in their eating and "love ethnic fusion cuisines."[86] Taste is also more important. They do not believe one has to trade out good taste to get good nutrition. In sum, Millennials demonstrate a preference for "unique and interesting food and beverage experiences, and they share these experiences with their social network."[87] They influence others. And others will likely follow. As Aurora Saulo, of the Department of Tropical Plant and Soil Sciences at the University of Hawai'i puts it: "They are trendsetters. They define future shopping and purchase behavior and have assumed their place in the consumer world. The Millennials are now a reliable barometer for tomorrow's food culture."[88]

85. National Peanut Board, "How Millennials are Changing How We Shop for Food," *National Peanut Board,* n.d., *https://www.nationalpeanutboard.org/news/how-millennials-are-changing-how-we-shop-for-food.htm.*

86. Dairy Farmers of America, "Notable Millennial Food Trends: What Do They Like To Eat?," *DFA Ingredient Solutions,* September 10, 2020, *https://dfaingredients.com/trends/millennial-food-trends/.*

87. Aurora Saulo, "Millennials and Food" (Hawai'i: College of Tropical Agriculture and Human Resources, 2016), Food Safety and Technology. *https://www.ctahr.hawaii.edu/oc/freepubs/pdf/FST-63.pdf*

88. *Ibid.*

BEYOND CONSCIOUS CONSUMERISM AND DEMOGRAPHICS

There are some trends that appear to cut across gender and demographic divides. We will take a look at those in the next chapter. Make no mistake. Most of the consumers of the food system are, in fact, food system outsiders. They are end users, but they do not participate significantly in the production, processing, or transportation of food products until they take them off the shelf, out of the box, or from across the takeout platform. They are not insiders. They are, however, looking to the inside of the system with greater diligence and a willingness to ask that system for something else.

To summarize here, it suffices to say that at least for the foreseeable future, consumers are going to be asking more and more questions about where their food comes from. Critically, it will not be farmers that answer them. It will be the food companies and retailers. And you can believe they will be prepared to give those consumers the answers they want to hear.

CHAPTER FIVE

READING THE FUTURE FOODIE TEA LEAVES

I will admit it. I personally believe that reading tea leaves is an unreliable way to predict the future. The practice involves sloshing pulverized tea particles around in a cup, draining off the liquid, and looking intently at what is left in the bottom for signs that foretell our destiny. Amazon is strewn with books offering to teach one about the art of tea leaf reading, some of which come with a special fortune telling cup and saucer to help you translate the spattering of grounds into deep insights about your love life or blatant personality flaws. The practice of reading tea leaves is called tasseography, which just goes to show you that something can still be stupid even if it has a fancy name and has been practiced for hundreds of years.

Some people who read this book will find the trends examined here to be equally as unsatisfying. I hope not. Keep the introduction to these consumer trends laid out in Chapter 4 in mind: the transition from foodies to good foodies, the rise of conscious consumerism, the role of gender and generational shifts, and the environment of abundance we are so blessed to have, particularly here in the United States.

Diving deeper, what are the key trends to watch? Which ones will be transcendental, lasting, and enduring over the next few decades? I will opine on this more in the closing chapter of this book. For now, take my word for it that the trends we see manifesting themselves in the food dynamic are the very same trends psychologists, anthropologists, and theologians see manifesting themselves in culture generally.

A CONSUMER ON THE GO

Turns out that, for all the advances in modern technology, most individuals and families still feel pressed for time.

Almost thirty years ago, the venerable American country group Alabama recorded a song entitled "I'm in a Hurry (and Don't Know Why)." The repeating chorus reads:

> *I'm in a hurry to get things done*
> *Oh I rush and rush until life's no fun*
> *All I really gotta do is live and die*
> *But I'm in a hurry and don't know why.*[89]

The song was a number one hit, as many Americans, including your author, identify closely with this "always rushing" phenomena.

89. Alabama Band, "I'm in a Hurry (And Don't Know Why)," YouTube Video, 0:01, posted February 18, 2017, *https://www.youtube.com/watch?v=15gT9HByEN4*.

If it was Alabama's hope that their outstanding contribution to country music would slow us down as a society, it seems it didn't work. Three decades later, we run around now as much as ever. At least we can post it on social media now.

This book is not the place to catalog the research of just why Americans are in such a hurry, but it suffices to say we are. Americans are known around the world for checking our watches, prodding the waitstaff with questions regarding how much longer before the food arrives, and for hating the wait at the Department of Motor Vehicles. Amazon would not offer to tell us our package was "only eight stops away" unless they knew it somehow calmed our foot tapping (or fed it).

The typical family with kids has to juggle getting those kids to one or more schools every day or homeschooling them, pressing to ensure the homework is done, carting budding athletes to sports practices and tournaments, not to mention navigating responsibilities like piano, church, dance, gymnastics, and the at least once weekly scrounging up of cash for the book fair, field trip, or afterschool activity. Add to this the fact that many working adults remain tethered to their workplace 24/7, and that a small but increasing share of households provide eldercare to someone in their family or household. Mix in a pet, preferably one that has to go to the vet often, an unreliable car, and a neighbor whose Amazon packages are consistently delivered to your home and you have the makings of some pretty hectic days. There is little wonder convenience is a factor in how people make food choices.

Don't take my word for it. Compare the frozen food choices in a grocery store today to what was there just thirty years ago. The days of a small freezer section featuring stocks of raw, frozen vegetables and a few pot pies are long gone. USDA's Economic Research Service has found that from the early 1980s to the middle of this decade, the annual supply of frozen fruit available for consumption grew by 61 percent.[90] Most of this growth was fueled by a doubling in demand for frozen berries, and most of those were destined for homemade smoothies. USDA's Agricultural Research Service touts its own contributions to making "frozen food that's freezer friendly."[91] We even have a national frozen food month. It's March. In case you were planning to celebrate.[92] Clarence Birdseye, the trapper turned frozen fish peddler largely considered to be the pioneer of frozen food, would be so proud.

There is, of course, an association that represents the interests of the frozen food industry on a national and even international scale. It is fittingly called the American Frozen Food Institute, and its capable president and CEO, Alison Bodor, recently summarized the continuing trend of lengthening frozen food aisles. "Strong sales data only tells part of the story," Bodor says. "Frozen foods align with the times we're living in, offering consumers nutrition, variety, ease of preparation and certainty at a moment we're needing it more than ever in our kitchens and on our tables."[93] She predicts the trend will continue for years to come.

NPD Group, an international market research firm, echoes Bodor's observations and notes that the clamor for convenience is also generational.

> *This is largely driven by increased responsibilities among a large Millennial population that has "grown*

---

90. "USDA Chart Detail," Chart Gallery, U.S. Department of Agriculture Economic Research Service, last modified July 26, 2017, *https://www.ers.usda.gov/data-products/chart-gallery/gallery/chart-detail/?chartId=84603.*

91. "USDA Frozen," Timeline, U.S. Department of Agriculture Economic Research Service, last modified February 14, 2018, *https://www.ars.usda.gov/oc/timeline/frozen/.*

92. My personal belief that nothing should still be frozen in the month of March is one of many reasons why I like living in the South. Diet Mountain Dew on every corner is another.

93. American Frozen Food Institute, "Why Frozen Foods Will Trend Up in 2021," American Frozen Food Institute, November 12, 2020, *https://affi.org/why-frozen-foods-will-trend-up-in-2021/.*

> *up" and is now in peak career and family-formation life stage . . . And as more Millennials reach a later life stage, manufacturers, retailers, and restaurant operators that offer time-saving solutions to busy consumers will be poised for success.*[94]

The drive for convenience and the need for speed don't end with the actual food we buy. They have also led to changes in how our kitchen gadgetry works. No longer content to brew a pot of coffee in eight to ten minutes, consumers either pop in the K-cup or hit the drive-through down the street. Don't feel like waiting in that drive-through line? Just order it on the app and it will be ready for you when you get there. Air fryers don't just cut down on fat. After all, who wants that? Their more enduring characteristic is that they cook food even faster than traditional Fry Daddy's.[95]

Why would you whip up a blender-made smoothie when you could prepare it in a Bullet? And while some of us may still remember the *shpt shpt shpt* sound emanating from the pressure cooker when our folks were canning vegetables, even more of us now know what an Instant Pot is. How much longer before kitchens come standard with flash freezers, or perhaps more to the point, flash thawers?

But these conveniences come at a cost. The food and the food gadgetry are more expensive. Surely that is holding back the shift? Perhaps not.

CMTC, California's Manufacturing Network, recently described four key drivers in the food and beverage supply chain, highlighting convenience at the top of the list. The Californians are, for better or worse, undeniable drivers of the overall direction of consumer trends.

94. NPD Group, "Consumers in 2020: 5 Trends to Watch," NPD Group, January 25, 2020, *https://www.npd.com/news/thought-leadership/2020/consumers-in-2020-5-trends-to-swatch-2/.*

95. Like the kind my wife wouldn't let me put on our wedding registry at Target over two decades ago. But I'm not bitter. Let frygones be frygones.

The size of the consumer market there is too big to ignore. CMTC points out that consumers are willing to put their money where what they buy for their mouth is.

> *A major competitive goal is to enhance product value through greater convenience. But such innovation typically comes with a premium price tag as a result of rising ingredient costs and new regulatory frameworks. Fortunately, more consumers are becoming receptive to paying a premium for food if there is a convenience factor to the product.*[96]

So exactly what are people buying? The National Frozen and Refrigerated Foods Association delineates the top five frozen department categories as ice cream, pizza, seafood, novelties, and complete meals.[97] Their research indicates that the frozen food section drives thirty-one trips to the grocery store per buying household annually and adds over $10 to shopping carts per trip. They also point out that half of U.S. households now have access to more than one freezer.[98]

Sure, we all love Smucker's Uncrustables, but today's consumer doesn't limit their search for convenience to the frozen food section. On-the-go consumption habits have also fueled the growth of other parts of the ready-to-eat food products market, including rice, numerous snacks, and even fried foods. Almost all grocery stores now offer heat-and-serve meals, and employee-owned Publix,

96. California Manufacturing Technology Consulting, "4 Consumer Trends Impacting the Food and Beverage Supply Chain," *CMTC California's Manufacturing Network,* June 28, 2017, *https://www.cmtc.com/blog/4-consumer-trends-impacting-food-and-beverage-supply-chain.*

97. Dave Fusaro, "Why Frozen Foods Are Hot Right Now," *Food Processing,* April 27, 2020, *https://www.foodprocessing.com/articles/2020/frozen-foods/.*

98. No more feeling guilty about my full-size garage refrigerator and freezer, which I purchased for $50 and two hours of work to pull it out of someone's basement. By the time the extraction was complete, I realized I was the sucker and my neighbors should have been paying me.

already a pioneer in fresh food offerings, now offers complete, hot, made-to-order entrées. Experts tell us the ready meal category is ripe for growth, and that those consumers will use this option to replace ready to cook and frozen meals.[99]

In sum, there is no denying that consumer convenience drives food purchases in stores, and that doesn't even address the rise of restaurants in the United States, the impact COVID has had on them, and the success of those that have pivoted (cringe) to supply takeout to the weary parent who wore out their best six home-cooked meals in the first thirty days of the pandemic.

As long as consumers' hectic lives are here to stay, so too is their reach for something convenient. But convenience alone is not enough.

WHOLE HEALTH EATING

We have known for generations that not all food sits the same within each of our gastrointestinal tracts. For me, onions are tough. Even tougher still is the fact that I actually like them and irrationally consume them despite knowing the carnage they will cause.

Some consumers' reactions to certain food ingredients include more than mere discomfort. In fact, in 2004, Congress responded to public health pressure around food allergen labeling and passed the Food Allergen Labeling and Consumer Protection Act. The Act requires that any FDA-regulated food containing one of the "Big 8" be specifically labeled to disclose as much.[100] Over 160 different

99. Elizabeth Crawford, "The ready meal category is ripe for growth and likely will pull consumers from meal kits and frozen," *FOODnavigator-usa.com,* July 31, 2017, *https://www.foodnavigator-usa.com/Article/2017/07/20/The-ready-meal-category-is-ripe-for-growth?utm_source=copyright&utm_medium=OnSite&utm_campaign=copyright.*

100. The eight foods identified by the law are: milk, eggs, fish, custacean shellfish, tree nuts, peanuts, wheat, and soybeans. "Food Allergies: What You Need to Know," Buy, Store & Serve Safe Food, U.S. Food and Drug Administration, last modified January 19, 2021, *https://www.fda.gov/food/buy-store-serve-safe-food/food-allergies-what-you-need-know.*

foods are known to cause allergic reactions, but these eight account for 90 percent of them. Not incidentally, as I wrote this book, the list grew to nine with the addition of sesame.[101]

It is one thing to avoid allergens or dodge that queasy feeling that comes from eating an eighth deviled egg in one sitting. And indeed, picking and choosing what foods are best for us is nothing new.[102] What is new is that today's food consumer is moving beyond mere avoidance of foods that make them feel bad or increasing their intake of those that make them feel better. Today's science offers the allure of an age of "personalized nutrition."

Personalized nutrition leverages technology in a way that allows a consumer to actually know—to a reasonable degree of scientific certainty—what food is best for their overall health and wellness.

Dr. Colin Kay, associate professor of translational nutrition at NC State University's Plants for Human Health Institute, has worked for years to catalog the metabolites released into our digestive tracts by certain foods as they are broken down in the body. According to a university publication chronicling his research, each of those metabolites can create different effects in the body. "Some may impact inflammation, while others may impact cardiovascular disease or diabetes."[103]

The point of Dr. Kay's research is to better understand the connection between food and health throughout the body, with the hope of fully deploying nutrition-based therapies in the future. In his

101. "S.578—FASTER Act of 2021," Legislation, Congress.gov, last modified April 23, 2021, *https://www.congress.gov/bill/117th-congress/senate-bill/578/text?q=%7B%22search%22%3A%5B%22S.+578%22%5D%7D&r=1&s=1*.

102. Although, as noted earlier, some of the historical recommendations of scientists like those responsible for producing the federal government's nutrition guidelines grow more comical as science evolves. For example, there was formerly a minimum butter intake recommendation, and then a federal tax on margarine to discourage its use.

103. North Carolina State University, "A Nutritional Shift: This Metabolome Library Might Change Our Understanding of Food and Health," *Plants for Human Health Institute,* August 9, 2019, *https://plantsforhumanhealth.ncsu.edu/2019/08/09/a-nutritional-shift-this-metabolome-library-might-change-our-understanding-of-food-and-health/*.

words, “this could lead to personalized nutrition, but not the faddist nutrition that leads someone to say, ‘I’m going to eat cantaloupe every day for 30 days.’”

Phil Mackie, managing partner of Foods & Beverages at Oakland Innovation, has observed: “It’s becoming easier for people to understand their own gut health and establish a link to their nutritional needs.” He predicts that “gut health” will be the area where the most innovation occurs in the personalized nutrition space. The popularity of gluten-free commitments is a manifestation of this prediction. You heard it here first: if the heart is the window into the soul, the gut is the telescope into better health.

While the science for this level of personalized nutrition is still not quite fully developed, that hasn’t stopped consumers from already clamoring for it, and food companies from hoping to offer it. The rise of nutrition and health coaches further illuminates this trend.[104] The irony here, of course, is that truly personalized nutrition cannot be mass produced because it is, well, personalized. Don’t tell that to the well-capitalized and well-subscribed disruptors who are already writing the book on nutrigenomics and DNA-driven supplement regimens. Today’s grocer and food companies are already offering several options that might be considered “personalized nutrition light,” and the science will fuel the desire for more.

104. Research and Markets, “United States Health Coaching Market Report 2021: Health Coaching has Emerged as a $7 Billion Service Market, with a Strong Growth Outlook,” *Research and Markets,* January 14, 2021, *https://www.globenewswire.com/en/news-release/2021/01/14/2158924/28124/en/United-States-Health-Coaching-Market-Report-2021-Health-Coaching-has-Emerged-as-a-7-Billion-Service-Market-with-a-Strong-Growth-Outlook.html.*

A MORE DIVERSE PALATE

As the United States grows ever more diverse, so does its palate. The 2020 U.S. Census reveals that the nation is diversifying even faster than predicted.[105] This alone is enough to drive growth in the ethnic food market, but evidence indicates that this is not the only factor. Food Dive, a publication that provides journalism and insight around the trends shaping the food industry, reports:

> *Asian and Middle Eastern flavors have struck a chord with consumers who are seeking new and intriguing items beyond the well-known standbys such as sushi, tempura, hummus, tahini and yogurt. Spicy flavors do well in the U.S., and many shoppers are exploring basic hot sauces as food makers highlight more authentic, ethnic flavors. Changing demographics are behind some of this trend, particularly as the purchasing power of the millennial demographic increases and companies target growing Hispanic and Asian populations. But millennials also are very interested in ethnic cuisine.*[106]

Recall that in Chapter 4, we mentioned that the desire to try new things and to use taste as an experience was a hallmark of Millennial culture. In other words, Millennials long to taste flavors well beyond their own ethnic backgrounds or even those of their friends and neighbors. Demand for Moroccan, Mediterranean and Middle Eastern, Greek, Spanish, Turkish, African, and even

105. William Frey, "The Nation Is Diversifying Even Faster Than Predicted, According to New Census Data," Brookings, July 1, 2020, *https://www.brookings.edu/research/new-census-data-shows-the-nation-is-diversifying-even-faster-than-predicted/*.

106. Patti Zarling, "Consumers Crave Authentic Ethnic Food—And Will Pay More," Food Dive, August 13, 2018, *https://www.fooddive.com/news/consumers-crave-authentic-ethnic-food-and-will-pay-more/529282/*.

Lebanese foods is growing. Our newfound fetish with sauces and dips is equally as impressive, even if one popular publication grossly refers to them as "food lube."[107]

Another factor driving ethnic food consumption is the very convenience trend mentioned above. Italian, Indian, Chinese, and other traditionally ethnic food choices already come in a variety of ready-to-eat or heat-and-serve forms. These frozen food choices have steadily improved over time. While we would likely all agree that frozen lasagna is not quite the same as homemade, we also would have to agree that it is still pretty darn good.

Like the other trends, a rising clamor for ethnic foods fits within our overall cultural trends. In other words, cultural curiosity has come to our dinner plates. Chances are, much of it is here to stay.

COVID'S ACCELERATION EFFECT AND OTHER SURPRISES

While it is too early to see precisely what the long-term impacts of COVID will be on the foodie movement, no one would seriously posit there are none. At some point during the pandemic, while growing nauseated from words like "unprecedented," which was of course entirely untrue, I heard an economist make the following observation: "Shocks to the system like this one have a way of accelerating trends that were already underway. Thus, trends that were already on the rise will rise more rapidly, and declining trends will spiral downward more quickly."[108]

This observation jibes with what it appears we are now observing in the food space. Initially, many families treated the COVID

107. Ben Paynter, "How America Became Obsessed with 'Food Lube'," *Men's Health,* September 3, 2020, *https://www.menshealth.com/nutrition/a33901460/food-lube-dips-dressing-sauces/.*

108. Mark Vitner, Wells Fargo Securities, LLC Managing Director & Senior Economist, "Ask the Experts: COVID-19 Economy—Slowdown or Shutdown?" (webinar, NC Chamber, Raleigh, North Carolina, April 16, 2020), *https://ncchamber.com/13994-2.*

lockdowns as a way to practice what they had grown accustomed to during snowstorms or other infrastructure crippling weather events. Popcorn sales skyrocketed. Snacking has returned with a vengeance. Murmurs of the "COVID 15," the fifteen pounds that could be attributed to the stay-at-home orders, were palatable—and visible. As the COVID dust begins to settle, and your author freely acknowledges that dust may never truly settle, the reemergence of a more health-conscious consumer proves this trend has staying power.

You might recall the early COVID shopping run on flour and baking supplies. This phenomenon was chronicled in numerous articles, but perhaps most convincingly, we saw it with our own eyes while trying to track down our own favorite brand. Megan McCarron wrote the following in an article for *The Eater* titled "The Year Flour Was King":

> *Big national brands and niche millers alike all flew off the shelves. Unlike toilet paper or beans, the flour wasn't being hoarded: Home baking across the country exploded, even when the grocery stores were barren and home bakers turned to pop-up restaurant grocers or split 50-pound bags.*[109]

This led us all to conclude that home baking was returning with a vengeance. Time will tell. What is more likely is that consumers will stick with doing the last five minutes of the baking at home, and avoid the fussy mess of sifting flour or waiting for yeast to rise. In other words, they will do more of what they were already doing pre-pandemic.

109. Meghan McCarron, "The Year Flour Was King," Easter, December 21, 2020, *https://www.eater.com/22178960/king-arthur-flour-supply-chain-baking-boom*.

In sum, there is no denying that COVID forced consumers to prepare and consume more food at home, and that home consumption is replacing some of the food formerly purchased at restaurants. But that preparation is still likely to be wed to convenience, health, and wider palates. Don't worry. The market is already hard at work attempting to meet these desires.

THE TAKEAWAYS

A complete presentation on the consumer trends shaping the food and agriculture system would fill this book and leave room for little else. It would also send the wrong message, and one that I believe ag and food leaders frequently succumb to. Namely, that the *only* thing driving the food system's metamorphosis is consumer behavior. As this book (hopefully) makes clear, nothing could be further from the truth. Even more to the point, outsiders who want to reform the food system are, in many cases, not necessarily responding to consumer behavior as much as they are trying to drive it.

Yet we cannot and should not ignore future consumers' expectations in the marketplace. Given that both insiders and outsiders are paying attention to consumers and their (sometimes admittedly insane, uninformed, or unrealistic desires), it is worth at least a passing glance.[110]

One last word or two about consumer trends. They can be counterintuitive. For example, even though more folks are shopping online, seeking out some level of convenience, and even picking up food that might be well on its way to already being prepared (without being processed), our shopping routines are anything but simple. Most shoppers have complex routines that are characterized by

110. I was on a Zoom call once and someone stated that figuring out consumers is like trying to figure out the mind of a serial killer. I'm not exactly sure what he meant. But it made an impression.

cross-shopping at multiple grocery stores.[111] The Food Marketing Institute is quick to point out that grocery shopping seems to be a "national pastime," a phrase typically reserved for baseball games, exorbitant Halloween budgets, and turkey at Thanksgiving. At least pre-COVID, data suggested that grocery shopping is something many Americans take pride in doing, and that they do it more frequently than they really need to. They may continue to do so, even if it is on their electronic device.

Admittedly, some consumer trends are, in fact, just fads. The already cooling clamor for rainbow bagels, cake pops (sorry, Starbucks), and pumpkin-spiced everything are, we can hope, good examples. But other trends will be more enduring, at least partly because they are a byproduct of our lifestyles and values. Of course, there are dozens of variables that influence food purchases. Culture, custom, economics, health, and geography, just to name a few. But are there trends that will not only shape the dynamics of the point of sale but also have the potential to trickle up to the farmer?

I believe the answer to that question is a resounding yes. That is why the research on what consumers want is so enlightening. The findings of those who earn a living navigating the desires and thoughts of consumers will continue to be key partners in navigating the farmer-versus-foodie debate.

The irony is that while grocers and food manufacturers focus intently on finding and exploiting that next consumer shift, farmers are relatively content to either ignore or outright criticize it. If I had a dollar for every time I saw a farmer shake his or her head upon learning of the latest consumer craze, I could afford to shop at Whole Foods. In my view, that is because those of us on the production side of agriculture (as opposed to those who face consumers

111. The Food Marketing Institute, U.S. Grocery Shopper Trends (The Food Marketing Institute: 2019), FMI Webinar PowerPoint Presentations. *https://www.fmi.org/docs/default-source/webinars/trends-a-look-at-today%27s-grocery-shopper-slides-pdf.pdf?sfvrsn=9d01576e_0.*

directly) frequently sum up shifts in the marketplace as mere blips and spurts, perhaps subconsciously adhering to the belief that the only reason cornbread and biscuit sales are flat is because many people have never had good cornbread and biscuits.

To the contrary, the consumer of tomorrow is not a younger version of the consumer of yesterday. There are ramifications down on the farm for that. The consumer of tomorrow is also not a nincompoop. They want what is best for their families but also maintain that they represent the best interests of the world and subsequent generations. They apply common sense notions to labels and generally believe that additives, genetic modifications, and pesticides sound bad and therefore must be bad. They want "clean," "pure," and "good" food, all words that have already been nabbed by organizations setting out to change the way the food system works. They also clamor for simplicity, committing to the theory that less is more when it comes to everything from ag inputs to food labeling and their food choices, even if they can't make that same commitment in other areas of life.

We in agriculture ignore these shifts and desires at our peril. The most painful part of it is seeing that in many ways, farmers and consumers often have the very same desires. The clowning crow that the food system is broken—and the hostility that accompanies it—nonetheless often prevents the minds of the willing farmer and consumer from meeting. That is a tragedy in slow motion. If Mel Gibson can figure it out, so can we.

CHAPTER SIX

BOTTOM LINES: OUTSIDE INVESTMENT IN AGRICULTURE

In 2019, I participated in Aimpoint Research's annual agri-food value chain industry-wide wargame in Nashville, Tennessee.[112] Calling this an eye-opening experience would be a bit like saying the apostle Paul developed an ocular twitch on the road to Damascus.[113] Like Paul, I apparently had scales over my eyes until a key moment in Aimpoint's wargame helped me see the light.

112. I did it again in 2021, and that time I won a tomahawk.

113. Paul was blind for three days, and ate nothing over this same period of time. Acts 9.

Aimpoint Research is a global, strategic intelligence firm with deep roots in military intelligence. Colonel (Retired) Mark Purdy, a senior vice president in the firm, is the former director of Wargame Operations at the U.S. Army War College in Carlisle, Pennsylvania. As Purdy explains, "The military has a long history of using wargames to solve complex problems and Aimpoint Research brings that success to the agri-food industry."

You might ask why former military intelligence officers and wargame experts would now, in their civilian lives, run a business that focuses on the future of the agri-food value chain. To them, the answer is simple: "Aimpoint Research operates with a core belief that food power is vital to maintaining U.S. national security."

To borrow from the United Kingdom's Security Service, MI5, society is "four meals away from anarchy." That's fewer than when Alfred Henry Lewis, an early twentieth century American journalist, described the same sentiment. In 1906, he said that there are "only nine meals between mankind and anarchy." Vladimir Lenin, the founder of the Russian Communist Party and leader of the Bolshevik Revolution whittled it down to this: "Every society is three meals away from chaos."

In Aimpoint's words, "The U.S. has taken for granted the power we have to both feed our citizens and produce enough surplus to feed nations around the world. When we look at the DIME (diplomatic, informational, military, and economic) elements of national power, the power of U.S. food on all four elements is huge. But there are constant threats to that power, and we want to help the U.S. agri-food industry ensure it remains competitive in a global market."

One way to do that is to bring key agriculture and food system leaders together to think deeply about the future of ag and food, test plausible scenarios and explore likely outcomes, and reveal those forces that will ultimately cooperate, compete, or be crushed. The participants in the wargame exercise include executives, leaders, and experts from the industry's top organizations representing the agri-food value chain, including financial services, ag inputs, farmers, policy experts, distributors, and processors. In 2019 and again in 2021, I joined this group of fifty to seventy key players recruited by Aimpoint CEO Brett Sciotto, already mentioned in Chapter 4.[114]

Wargaming necessarily involves tension. During the 2019 exercise, I had been assigned to "Team Farmers," which we subsequently renamed to make sure our opponents knew we were serious competitors.[115] Sciotto and his colleagues had used the wargaming process to introduce key stressors within the agri-food value chain. Our job was to plan our reactions and return to the wargame table to duke it out with other groups of players in the room. Importantly, the breakout groups—the teams—could approach each other throughout the day to form alliances and partnerships, something we later wished we had done more strategically.

The Power of Partnership—and the Peril of Independence

Without spelling out the details of the otherwise confidential session, Team Farmers concluded that we would develop and deploy our own technology to respond to one of Sciotto's (not so) surprise stressors. We could have approached another team and worked with them to create the needed technology, or we could have even admitted that we would outsource that task to the market generally. But we didn't. Instead, we took the position that we would do what farmers know how to do best: innovate and act with fierce independence to meet the next challenge. After all, it was farmers that figured out they could duct tape cows' ears to keep them from freezing off during

114. Sciotto and his team are undoubtedly among an elite group of key thought leaders on the future of agriculture and food in the United States.

115. Unfortunately, upon reflection, the name was not appropriate for all audiences and I am thus reluctant to mention it here.

uncharacteristically harsh winters.[116] Surely Team Farmers could stridently navigate the next need for technological advancement thrown at us during a fictitious wargame exercise.

The problem here was that we couldn't. Not without a little help from our friends. And that was a fact Captain Sciotto and Colonel Purdy were all too ready to make clear to us. We put our best "we are farmers, we feed the world" argument forward, but they didn't buy it. Despite our protestations and my best Matlock-style arguments (minus the seersucker suit, and perhaps that is what made the difference), we lost that round.

Note the double whammy here. We lost partly because we truly did not have the time, know-how, or resources to develop the industrial science we would need to react to the circumstances presented in the wargame. But recall that we could have realigned or partnered with other key agriculture and food sector players, which of course we had decided not to do. It was our own hubris and independent streak that ultimately doomed us.

The point here is that the Aimpoint Research leaders did for me precisely what I hope this chapter does for you. That experience sobered me to the reality that in many senses, farmers are the adopters of new ag invention, not the sole progenitors of it. The large-scale innovations that will drastically alter the future of the sector in the coming years will certainly have to show their worth on real farms. And farmers will have a role in their development. But in some instances, they will develop in spite of, and not because of, farmers' participation in that development.

Let me leave no doubt. Farmers are participating directly in the development of the next-generation technology that we will use to feed ourselves and others. We all know farmers who host trial plots. We also know farmers who might be fully employed at a

116. Michael Hirtzer, et al., "U.S. Ranchers Are Using Duct-Tape to Keep Cows' Ears From Freezing Off," *Fortune,* February 17, 2021, *https://fortune.com/2021/02/17/us-farmers-cold-weather-duct-tape-cows-ears-freezing-off/.*

major agricultural company or work for their respective department of agriculture or the extension service, but who continue to actively farm privately for additional income. There are even rock stars like Joy Parr Drach, who is the CEO of Advanced Animal Diagnostics but also a cattle farmer herself. No doubt her farm experiences relate directly to the work AAD is doing to provide farmers with more rapid and advanced, you guessed it, animal diagnostics. In Joy's case, one of those diagnostic tools detects subclinical mastitis in dairy cows, which can give dairy farmers a major leap on their attempts to control the disease.

Note, however, that even Joy has relied on the power of partnership. She has leveraged relationships outside of her own farm to create multiple products that show extraordinary promise for mass commercialization. In fact, in a recent *Successful Farming* interview, Joy counsels the farming and ranching community as follows: "If we are going to succeed, we need more innovation. That takes farmers and ranchers getting involved with innovators to provide feedback and to help shape the technology we develop."[117] Read closely, that is not a call for farmers to hunker down and do more on their own. It is the opposite. Farmers—as insiders—have to learn how to leverage the outsider investors who are looking to transform farming and food.

As discerning consumers and an international stage demand more and more from agriculture, farmers will increasingly rely on outsiders for the development of the tools and technology that maintain their safety, efficiency, sustainability, and profitability. One cannot duct tape their way to genetic engineering, traceability, or carbon capture monitoring. Deeper pockets and well-heeled investors will either become partners or work around farmers to give the

117. Laurie Bedord, "Q&A: Joy Parr Drach, Advanced Animal Diagnostics," *Successful Farming,* February 21, 2020, *https://www.agriculture.com/news/business/q-a-joy-parr-drach-advanced-animal-diagnostics.*

market what it is looking for. Outside investment in agriculture is just one more force altering the future of food and farming.

I'M AN OUTSIDE INVESTOR . . . AND I'M HERE TO HELP

So who are these investors? Why are they attracted to American agriculture? My concern is that it appears many of them are lining up with the Humpty Dumptyers who believe we need to "fix farming." Joy agrees with me. Regarding the latest entrants into ag investment, she observes via e-mail:

> *The throng of investors entering to 'transform agriculture,' as you and they say, reminds me of the reaction to 'I'm from the government and I'm here to help you.' I grew up surrounded by corn fields on a farm not too far from Peoria, IL where President Eisenhower gave the speech that included his famous quote: 'Farming looks mighty easy when your plow is a pencil, and you're a thousand miles from the corn field.' Some of that crop of investors you reference have really valuable experience to help agtech startups. But many remind me of that quote. They don't understand the complexities of what it takes to grow food, fuel and fiber and get it safely to the point of consumption, and that creates opportunity for unintended negative consequences of their actions. One example involves a company touting carbon credit technology that would, to implement, force me to rip up ground that we've been no tilling already.*

It may not matter. These investors are putting their money where their mouths are. Some are traditional agriculture investors, including companies with large agricultural product portfolios and massive research and development budgets. Other investors know very little about farming in the traditional sense, yet they fund small scale startups that operate independently or with a small cadre of farmers until they have established proof of concept.

Sometimes, investors are just flat wrong about agriculture. I was disappointed to hear Peter Thiel say, in a conversation at Harvard Kennedy School's Institute of Politics with Niall Ferguson, that agriculture's leaps in productivity stopped in the 1980s.[118] His take is that agricultural production has "stalled out" in the last thirty years. This is simply inaccurate. In fact, annual agricultural productivity has increased over 2 percent a year since the 1980s, at the very same time that inputs, labor, and land use have generally decreased.[119]

Why All the Fuss?

At both large scale and small, my hypothesis here is that the arrival of the newest entrants into the ag investment space is largely driven by the notion that those already engaged in this space are not innovating fast enough. Some of them may be showing up because they read that the sector is victim to the "underutilization of data."[120]

118. Harvard Kennedy School's Institute of Politics, "A Conversation with Peter Thiel and Niall Ferguson," YouTube Video, 14:36, posted April 5, 2021, *https://www.youtube.com/watch?v=vyxqlJTPIJY*; *https://iop.harvard.edu/forum/conversation-peter-thiel-and-niall-ferguson*.

119. Eric Njuki, "A Look at Agricultural Productivity Growth in the United States, 1948–2017," U.S. Department of Agriculture, July 29, 2021, *https://www.usda.gov/media/blog/2020/03/05/look-agricultural-productivity-growth-united-states-1948-2017*.

120. In 2015, McKinsey Global Institute famously dubbed "agriculture and hunting" as the least digitized sector among a group of twenty-two different key business classes across the economy. The same report indicates negative growth in this sector 2009–2015 and states that agriculture and hunting only account for 1 percent of the GDP and 1 percent of the employment share, numbers that will shock many of the agricultural leaders who consistently tout the contributions of farmers to the economy. There's more

Still others believe food holds greater promise for human health and that we have merely scratched the surface for what we could, with additional investment, accomplish with food as medicine. And finally, while those who occupy the space may not want to admit it, some are here just because they've heard that ag investments are cool and everybody is doing it. One investment advisor recently quipped that one of his clients said, "We support sustainability development in agriculture, whatever that means."

The recent rise in ag and food tech investment is at least partly attributable to a historical lag of investment when compared to other industries over the last thirty to fifty years. In some sense, we are finally catching up. COVID also shocked the traditional assumption that 50 percent of the American food dollar is spent away from home. Where many of us worried about that rerouting, others saw investment opportunity. The chaos of COVID purportedly revealed massive vulnerabilities in the food chain—an oft-repeated observation that has little to do with reality. More accurately, it merely accelerated trends and vulnerabilities that were already present.

Still others believe they are reading the tea leaves on where consumers want to go, and believe they can beat the traditional investors in developing the products that will meet those desires. Corporate responsibility goals also come into play, and have launched many dollars on a hunt for a more sustainable agriculture sector. Make no mistake, investors—particularly outside investors—believe disruption in the ag sector is long overdue, even if they think so for a variety of reasons.

---

to the mosh pit of numbers thrown around regarding agriculture's contribution to the economy—perhaps enough for another book. McKinsey & Company, "Digital America: A Tale of the Haves and Have-Mores" (McKinsey Global Institute: 2015), McKinsey & Company Media. *https://www.mckinsey.com/industries/technology-media-and-telecommunications/our-insights/digital-america-a-tale-of-the-haves-and-have-mores*.

So Who Are They?

Without debate, the most dominant marketplace analysis of the modern-day flow of capital into agriculture innovation is the data and insight provided by AgFunder. While not the largest of its kind, AgFunder refers to itself as a "new kind of venture capital firm," with the mission of investing in "bold and impactful technologies rapidly transforming our food and agriculture system."[121] In existence since 2013 and based in Silicon Valley (note that—it's not the San Joaquin Valley or Chicago, Indianapolis, or St. Louis, it's where the microchip and sourdough bread makers are), AgFunder is widely considered to be a reliable source of information on where venture capital is flowing in the agriculture and food system.

In analyzing the chatter around ag investment, one must assume return on investment is front and center. Just beyond that, however, lurks a lot of conversation about addressing the Humpty Dumptyism in the food and farming sector that everyone outside of ag likes to bemoan. Entities like AgFunder openly tout their desire to be about the business of "transforming our food and agriculture system." AgFunder's opening pitch reads:

> *Driven by shifts in eating habits, population growth, climate change, and failing soils, our food and agriculture industry faces moonshot-sized challenges. Agri-FoodTech entrepreneurs are stepping up to solve these problems by harnessing the most advanced technologies. From plant-based protein, gene-editing, drones and indoor farming to satellite imaging, precision farming, and computational*

121. "AgFunder," Why FoodTech and AgTech, AgFunder, last modified November 30, 2021, *https://agfunder.com/*.

biology, founders are driving radical transformation in our food and agriculture system with technology.[122]

While not necessarily an admonition that agriculture is hurling toward a catastrophic collision with destiny, there is still some sense here that the cavalry has arrived to fund the efforts to save it.[123]

Most investors in the agriculture space—those at AgFunder included—merely want to improve the current system and see plenty of opportunities to do so. The tension I'm highlighting—and which I want to highlight respectfully—is that, unlike the investment community, much of the farming community thinks conservatively about the need for transformational breakthroughs. This is largely because they believe the system is already doing such an extraordinary job. (Which, of course, it is.) In fact, when I address a room full of farmers and talk about some of the mind-boggling innovation referenced in this chapter, about half of them roll their eyes. I am surprised there isn't already a country song entitled "I Don't Need Fixin'." If there were, most farmers would be able to sing along. What sometimes gets lost in translation is that bright minds—with investment behind them—can improve a system that many of us believe is already extraordinary.

Each year, AgFunder produces their AgriFoodTech Investment Report, typically touting the year-over-year double-digit growth of startup investment in the agrifoodtech space around the world. While "agrifoodtech" is not all inclusive in terms of dollars chasing opportunity in the farming and food equity game, this newly coined term is meant to signal that the solutions it underwrites operate at

122. *Ibid.*

123. According to AgFunder, these investors are attempting to address the following challenges: food waste, CO2 emissions, chemical residues and run-off, drought, labor shortages, health and sugar consumption, opaque supply chains, distribution inefficiencies, food safety and traceability, farm efficiency and profitability, and unsustainable meat production. It sort of makes you wonder what they will do with all their spare time.

both ends of the spectrum, from farm to fork as the saying goes. Today, agrifoodtech investment touts a more holistic view of the entire value chain, from agricultural production to consumption.

In the words of their 2021 report, for agrifoodtech, "it's been a blow-out year."[124] Looking back to 2020, a year in which the entire developed world was rocked by the COVID-19 pandemic, startups raised over $26 billion. This was a 15.5 percent year-over-year increase, and AgFunder predicted this number would rise even more as additional information for deals struck in 2020 came to the fore. A rise to $30 billion in investment in 2021 (which as of the time of writing was within the trajectory) would represent skyrocketing growth in this discipline: 34.5 percent growth over 2019, which was also a banner year. The growth in agrifoodtech is even more staggering when tracked longitudinally back to 2012. The current numbers are over eight times their 2012 amount.

BIG IDEAS . . . AND VENTURES

A lengthy dive into the work those funders are supporting is not possible given the space constraints here, although it makes for interesting reading. Just to give you a quick survey of some of the stunning possibilities, a company called Tevel is developing drone-like autonomous fruit pickers, which presumably never fall off the apple ladder. Atomo! has created a molecular-built coffee that is delicious, but which doesn't contain any actual . . . you guessed it . . . coffee. Their website invites you to meet the "brainiacs behind the magic," which is well worth your time to do.[125] The Paris-born Ÿnsect has perfected state-of-the-art insect farms, which ultimately offer "premium, high-value ingredients for pets, fish, plants, and

124. AgFunder, *AgFunder AgriFoodTech Investment Report* (AgFunder Research: 2021), AgFunder. *https://research.agfunder.com/2021/2021-agfunder-global-report.pdf.*

125. "Atomo: Molecular Cold Brew," Home, Atomo Coffee, last modified ___, 2021, *https://www.atomocoffee.com/.*

[. . . wait for it . . .] human beings."[126] So much for complaining that there's a bug in your food.

Not to mention Pivot Bio's microbial nitrogen technology, mustard seed derived pesticides, and an unfolding view of food as medicine that health insurers are sure to love. Even companies operating in traditional spaces along the agri-food value chain have attracted massive amounts of capital. Lineage Logistics, run by a cracker-jack crew of go getters trying to transform the cold storage chain, was the landing place of more outside investment in 2020 than any other other agrifoodtech venture referred to in the AgFunder report. COVID and America's ensuing interest in supply chain "resiliency" has only made them more popular.

Like AgFunder, another key player is Finistere Ventures. They also partner with companies seeking capital in the agritech value domain. Their landing page includes some of the same optimistically transformational language found elsewhere in the ag venture capital funding discipline: "We help ambitious founders transform food and agriculture. Since 2006, we've provided growth capital to partner with the best and boldest companies that are helping feed the world sustainably."[127] All that's missing from these mission-minded calls for repentance is the music. They already have the offering plate-passing part down pat.

Finistere produces their own annual report, relying on a slightly different dataset than AgFunder, but which generally reveals the same trends and deal growth. In the introductory letter to the report, Finistere co-founder and partner Arama Kukutai hints that notwithstanding the explosive growth, the party is just getting started. In his words: "There is strong indication that the race for innovation access is heating up and creating an exciting stage for agrifood investing as

126. "Ÿnsect," Home, Ÿnsect, last modified March 26, 2021, *https://www.ynsect.com/en/*.

127. "Finistere Ventures," Home, Finistere Ventures, last modified November 11, 2021, *https://finistere.com/*.

we move into the next decade."[128] Read carefully, Kukutai appears to be suggesting that there may be more money looking for promising innovation than there is promising innovation looking for money.

This view is confirmed by a brief conversation I had over chicken wings at a football game with Tom Mastrobuoni, the chief investment officer for Big Idea Ventures. Big Idea Ventures is a venture capital fund that invests in and accelerates top performers in what they call the "new food space." Mastrobuoni was a founding partner/chief financial officer for Tyson Ventures and has led investments in Beyond Meat, Clear Labs, FoodLogiQ, Future Meat Technologies, Memphis Meats, MycoTechnology, New Wave Foods, and Tovala. In a recent conversation regarding the capital looking for innovation in food and agriculture, Mastrobuoni shared that "you have to know someone" to get in.

The Finistere Ventures 2020 AgriFood Tech Investment Review is not even subtle about the fact that investors view agriculture and the food value chain as an area that calls out for reform. In their view, investors are not waiting for that reform to occur at the policy level, they are looking to effectuate it themselves. Finistere observes that the innovation revolution in agriculture is across the board: "The attraction for investors of disrupting massive TAMs [total addressable markets] fueled increases in investment across all stages and segments." The point, then, is that investors view both the size of the market and the need for innovation in the market as just too promising to ignore. It is yet another indication that the mantra that the food system is broken—or at least ripe for significant repair—continues to fuel outside interest in and influence on the sector.

---

128. Finistere Ventures LLC, *2020 Agrifood Tech Investment Review* (Finistere Ventures: 2020), Finistere Ventures. *https://finistere.com/wp-content/uploads/2021/04/Finistere-Ventures-2020-AgriFood-Tech-Investment-Review.pdf.*

THE RISE OF CORPORATE CONSCIOUSNESS

Another key observation about the recent agriculture investment craze is that part of the driving force here comes from the view that funds dedicated to disruptive efforts within the agri-food value chain are particularly attractive for investors looking to achieve certain ESG goals. ESG goals, typically defined as "environmental, social, and governance" criteria, are one way socially conscious investors screen potential investments. In each of the three pillars, the view abounds that ag has much more work to do. It is a huckleberry ripe for picking.

Longtime agriculture industry guardian Charlie Arnot, who is the CEO of a national not-for-profit organization dedicated to building consumer trust and confidence in today's food system, shared that agriculture and agribusiness are woefully unprepared for the ESG investment, and thus the accompanying ESG oversight onslaught. Most concerning is the observation that the costs of conforming to ESG deliverables may not be equitably distributed in the food value chain. Production agriculture could be saddled with much of the costs, but not participate in the premium being offered for that work. In Charlie's words, "the VP of 'make it go away' likely doesn't fully understand the commitments he or she is making and that they will have bottom line impacts on the farm."

In November of 2020, the United States Forum for Sustainable and Responsible Investment produced a biennial report that tracks how U.S. asset-management firms and institutional asset owners deploy sustainable investment strategies.[129] There were at least two striking revelations in the report that are relevant here. First, sustainable investing assets now account for one dollar of every three of the total assets under professional management in the U.S.

129. US SIF, "The US SIF Foundation's Biennial 'Trends Report' Finds That Sustainable Investing Assets Reach $17.1 Trillion," *US SIF: The Forum for Sustainable and Responsible Investment,* November 16, 2020, *https://www.ussif.org/blog_home.asp?Display=155.*

In 2019, that amounted to $17.1 trillion. Thus, there is plenty of ESG money looking for a home. Second, sustainable agriculture is viewed as a primary target landing pad for many of these investors.[130] This is a view shared by the U.S. Farmers and Ranchers in Action (USFRA), a national network of farmer- and rancher-led associations who have come together to push for a revolution in climate-smart agriculture.[131] Concomitantly, technologies that reduce greenhouse gas emissions—or better yet sequester carbon—that address increasingly constricting labor challenges, or that can fit into the food-for-health category are all magnetic for ESG investors.

Chuck Connor, a long-time D.C. advocate for the National Council of Farmer Cooperatives, notes that farmers will feel the pinch of ESG as "regulation through retail." Food companies have tight margins and care deeply about retail sales growth. Many simply will not be able to resist the temptation to say and do whatever is needed to keep their revenue growth—and the ESG capital—coming. Precisely how this will impact farmers is something we are going to learn in relatively short order.

Lest you think ESG investing is a fad or that it will come and go without leaving a mark, I bring to your attention two recent observations. The first is a digital advertisement I saw recently that promoted a degree in "sustainable finance." You can get an undergraduate degree in it, a master's, or even become "certified."[132] I'm sure there's a doctorate of sustainable finance somewhere. Not a sign that this is going away.

---

130. Debbie Carlson, "Sustainable Agriculture Is the Next Way ESG Investors Can Fight Climate Change," *Market Watch,* March 27, 2021, *https://www.marketwatch.com/story/7-ways-for-esg-investors-to-profit-from-sustainable-agriculture-11616600205.*

131. U.S. Farmers & Ranchers in Action, *Transformative Investment in Climate-Smart Agriculture* (U.S. Farmers & Ranchers in Action: 2021), U.S. Farmers & Ranchers in Action. *https://usfarmersandranchers.org/wp-content/uploads/2021/02/USFRA-Transformative-Investment-Report.pdf*.

132. "Sustainable Finance Institute," Home, Sustainable Finance Institute, last modified December 2, 2021, *https://sfini.org/.*

The second observation is that government is going to accelerate this trend as opposed to belabor it. In my view, that is interesting because government almost always trails the private sector in addressing market shifts. By the time this book is published, the Securities and Exchange Commission will likely have published more on its plans for a unified ESG disclosure system.[133] There's wide agreement that the SEC will start with climate, but their focus could easily spiral into more. Employee diversity. Executive diversity. Even risks from cyberattacks. Some ESG mandates are even being implemented at the state level. Eventually, more reporting uniformity and accountability will surface, whether in a system policed by the SEC or otherwise, and ESG will become a floor, not a differentiator. I will leave it up to you to determine whether agricultural companies are ready for this level of scrutiny. The obvious concern is that this will lead to the goodification and the badification of agriculture enterprises. Rest assured, those labeled "bad," or ESG-deficient, will have a harder time accessing capital. Sales may be harder to come by, too. ESG companies will buy only from the good ones—or, more accurately, from the ones that can best articulate how good they are.

Speaking of that ability to articulate, Tim Hammerich is a strategic communications consultant who produces and hosts the Future of Agriculture podcast, which I highly recommend. Tim is no stranger to story and storytelling. A former National FFA President, he has spent many hours behind a microphone, but he also understands commodities and the commodity marketplace. During a recent conversation, Tim explained the appeal of the ESG "story." "The way outside investors in ag raise money from their limited partners is to take the story—the story of agriculture and food production—and identify the villain in that story. Then, of

133. Recommendation of the SEC Investor Advisory Committee Relating to ESG Disclosure (May 21, 2020), Securities and Exchange Commission, Washington, D.C., *https://www.sec.gov/spotlight/investor-advisory-committee-2012/esg-disclosure.pdf.*

course, they and their investors can play the part of hero themselves by counteracting the villain." In their story, "the villain is sometimes modern production agriculture."

Of course, not all the money flowing into agriculture innovation is new or from outside. Traditional ag companies—and even some farmers themselves—are investing heavily in next-generation agriculture and food technology. In fact, many of the startup companies tracked in the above-referenced reports are funded by dollars from entities any American farmer would recognize, although their venture funds likely operate with different nomenclature. Adding to that, the venture capital board community is stacked with folks reared in one of the many multinational firms that dominated ag innovation for decades. Still, new but serious food venture capital players like Mastrobuoni (mentioned above) and Dr. Ryan Bethencourt, posit that most of the innovation is occurring in some of the smallest labs and startups. Elsewhere, particularly in the food space, what we are seeing from more traditional players is really just innovation illusion. The fifteenth novelty flavor of our favorite cereal is not really a disruptive breakthrough in improving the food system. It's arguably taking it backward.

The numbers juiced by recent entrants must also be kept in perspective. While the numbers mentioned above may initially raise eyebrows, the USFRA's 2021 Transformative Investment Report points out that total assets under management in the agricultural value chain (from institutional, retail, and government investors) borders on $1 trillion.[134] This observation makes the most recent investment levels look small, but the point here is that this money is underwriting disruption and financing breakthroughs, not funding

134. U.S. Farmers & Ranchers in Action, *Transformative Investment in Climate-Smart Agriculture* (U.S. Farmers & Ranchers in Action: 2021), U.S. Farmers & Ranchers in Action, p. 54. *https://usfarmersandranchers.org/wp-content/uploads/2021/02/USFRA-Transformative-Investment-Report.pdf.* This report is an extraordinarily well-constructed deeper dive into the dollars flowing—and those that could still come if certain reforms were adopted—into agriculture.

Billy Bob Beamer's operating loan or new refrigerators for the new Greengrocer down the street.

DISRUPTORS DON'T COME TO TELL YOU YOU'RE DOING A GOOD JOB

It is easy to be enamored by the shiny objects like the bugs-for-lunch venture, but there are stronger lessons to learn here, particularly within the construct of the farmers versus foodies lens. First, capital is being attracted by promises of disruption and improvement within the global food and ag industry. What these investors are doing is akin to a developer seeking out structurally sound real estate in a bad part of town. They intend to improve the neighborhood, and they feel strongly the neighborhood needs to be gentrified. In other words, investors have bought in—literally—to the notion that the real estate in our part of town must be renovated, or less charitably, that it needs to be razed. One Canadian fund proudly limits its investments to "responsible agriculture," which slyly begs the question of whether everything else is "irresponsible" agriculture. Very few of the newest disruptors that are pouring money into the future of food and agriculture come from traditional agriculture backgrounds. They are, instead, outsiders. Their views of the state of the current food system are shaped more by the belief that it must be reformed than by any idyllic childhood farm experiences.

Second, they anticipate significant returns. It might be easy to conclude that today's farm- and food-system investor is merely here to help. That their entrance into this area is altruistic. That would obviously be a mistake. They believe there are beat-the-market ROIs that can be achieved from dumping cash into the ag world, and they believe they know something the traditional players don't. Many of them tout a "can't lose" mentality when pointing to the dynamics that make ag investment attractive: a growing world population, diminishing resources, climate change, and more discerning consumers. It almost goes without saying that much of this investment is occurring inside the United States, which speaks volumes to our ability to innovate and protect intellectual property, but we are not the only country that is home to this burgeoning phenomenon.[135]

The third takeaway is that capital is generally not viewed as the key barrier to the development of the new technologies that will rout traditional agriculture. Louisa Burwood-Taylor, editor of AgFunder News, and the AgFunder team point out that this genre of investment is enjoying a "widening spectrum of venture capital investors."[136] Sounds like we are just getting started.

One more observation, and the most relevant to the overarching theme of this book: this capital isn't coming from the farm community. Just as the wargame exercise demonstrated, there are other folks in the sandbox, and they probably have never driven a tractor or combine, although I doubt they would be intimidated by the idea.[137] That said, these new players can do things aggies can't, and many of them will be successful.

Free Money

A chapter on outside investment in agriculture would be incomplete without at least mentioning the philanthropic largesse that is pouring

135. India and Israel, for example, are also home to at least a fair share of disruptive investment.

136. AgFunder, AgFunder AgriFoodTech Investment Report (AgFunder Research: 2021), AgFunder. *https://research.agfunder.com/2021/2021-agfunder-global-report.pdf.*

137. Did you know that FFA still sponsors tractor- and truck-driving competitions? It's no joke. Backing a trailer within a set of cones while discerning judges (and your ag teacher) look on is almost as frightening as backing a piece of farm equipment under a barn shelter while your farmer father looks on disapprovingly. Not that I have any experience with that. Teach a GPS tractor to back a hammermill under a dirt-floored lean-to without hitting the haphazardly stacked hoes on one side and the old buckets of spent motor oil on the other. Then I will be impressed.

into efforts to transform the food system. This topic deserves its own chapter, and could probably fill an entire book. My effort here will be merely to introduce it and hope that others with greater insight can dive deeper over time.

The Food & Agriculture program at the Schmidt Family Foundation—think Google—focuses on the programmatic goal of "reforming" animal agriculture. The Schmidt Foundation openly expresses its disgust with CAFOs, and through its "11th Hour Project" it has funded environmental networks that attack them. There's the Greenbaum Foundation, Patagonia, and the Stray Dog Institute. Sustainable Agriculture and Food Systems Funders, out of Santa Barbara, California, supports "just and sustainable food and agriculture systems," and is doing its part to back farmers "off the herbicide treadmill."[138] They leverage their own philanthropic contributions and investment dollars to create a "vibrant, just, and sustainable food system," which is apparently very different from what we have now.[139] I have to mention the Grace Communications Foundation, home of meatless Monday and the movie *The Meatrix*. There are others, including funders of endowed programs at premier academic institutions not known for their work on counseling modern farmers (because they don't counsel modern farmers).

My favorite example of philanthropic engagement in agriculture is the well-known Rockefeller Foundation. A little-known fact is that Norman Borlaug was a Rockefeller Foundation staffer when he planted the seeds of the Green Revolution. Consider the irony, then, of the foundation's more recent efforts to paint our modern food system as unsustainable and unfit for the twenty-first century.[140]

138. "Sustainable Agriculture and Food Systems Funders," Home, SAFSF, last modified October 8, 2020, *https://www.agandfoodfunders.org/*.

139. "Impact Investing in Food and Ag," Featured Work, SAFSF, last modified June 23, 2021, *https://www.agandfoodfunders.org/featured-work/impact-investing-in-food-and-ag/*.

140. "True Cost of Food: Measuring What Matters to Transform the U.S. Food System," Report, Rockefeller Foundation, last modified November 15, 2021, *https://www.*

"Our food system is failing us, and too few people understand the true cost of the food we consume, and lack clear incentives to change a system that is costing us dearly." In their view, the current system is filled to the brim with systemic inequities and fails to prioritize "human welfare and environmental health." They have devoted big dollars to discern the "true costs" of our food system, and begin their report on these efforts with a chapter entitled "An Urgent Need to Transform the U.S. Food System." I've read it. It is not, in any sense, a rousing endorsement of the American agriculture and food system.

Perhaps these efforts are well-intentioned. But that doesn't mean the outcomes they seek match those sought by the men and women currently engaged in production agriculture. Shame on us if we ignore the field of philanthropy and its impact on the future of our sector. And shame on someone reading this if they don't research and write more about it.

SO WHAT?

All of this leads to the inescapable conclusion that the ag and food value chain is, at least at the moment, occupying a position that is downhill from the investment waterfall, with everything from traditional ag lenders to activist investors on the precipice above. Corey Rosenbusch, who now serves as president and CEO of the venerable Fertilizer Institute, suggested to me that the agriculture sector may need to open advocacy shops in New York City. He's right. Someone needs to educate this powerful class of investors. Although I don't think that's what most people think of when they hear the phrase "Wall Street lobbyists."

---

rockefellerfoundation.org/report/true-cost-of-food-measuring-what-matters-to-transform-the-u-s-food-system/.

The rising inflow of capital into ag led one thoughtful investing firm managing principal to recently ask whether this money is a blessing or a curse.[141] To me, it is not even close. Bring on the new comrades. We need their help. In fact, we share some of the same frustrations. In a 2020 Farm Foundation Forum webinar entitled "Investing in Agriculture—What Does the Future Hold," Kiersten Stead, managing partner for DCVC and formerly of Monsanto Growth Ventures, spoke to some of the challenges that plague this group of optimistic, socially conscious investors. Stead points out that new arrivals in the ag investment community are sometimes surprised to learn the deployment of the breathtaking, science-based, problem-solving improvements they helped bring to fruition can still be thwarted by those espousing "romanticized or idealistic notions of agriculture." Preach, Sister Stead! What good is an emerging technology if the consuming public (or market protectionists across the pond) won't let us deploy it? Welcome to the team, venture capitalists. Grab a jersey and helmet and get on the field.

Back one more time to the personal lesson of the 2019 wargame, this time pondering what outside investors are more than happy to fund. Bugs and other "alternative proteins" for lunch. Imagery analytics. Metabolic engineering. Robotic or fully autonomous harvesting technology. Digitalization. Cell-based meat. Resource stewardship. Biotechnology. Genetics. Therapeutic chemistry. Microbial revolutions. Functional foods. The list grows impressively longer every day. As the facilitators of the Aimpoint exercise made clear to me, farmers likely won't be the ones to develop or even to

141. Jim Budzynski, "Outside Agriculture Investors: Blessing or Curse?" *AgFunder News*, July 21, 2017, *https://agfundernews.com/outside-agriculture-investors-blessing-or-curse.html*.

fund the development of the next-era breakthroughs here.[142] But they will need to partner with the outsiders that do. Even if some of those outsiders showed up with their pocketbooks only because they think many of today's farm and food system insiders are getting it wrong.

142. To be sure, many farmers will continue to scoff at some of the ideas the Agriculture Navy Seals are attempting to execute. And in some cases, they will prove to be correct—not all of these ideas will have staying power. But history is strewn with stories of inventors who were told there was no use for their inventions.

CHAPTER SEVEN

DECLINING POLITICAL CLOUT

While serving as Secretary of Agriculture Sonny Perdue's Chief of Staff, I was fortunate enough to work in the Jamie L. Whitten Building, CENTCOM for USDA, at 1400 Independence Avenue in Washington, D.C.[143] I was even more fortunate to have a parking spot just a few steps from the front door, on what insiders called "the apron." On more than one occasion, I took time before scampering in to read the quotes that adorned the attic panels just atop the Corinthian columns that donned the main entrance. One was from Saint Paul, another from President Lincoln, and a third from Washington. Good luck finding the text of those quotes on the internet.

The most succinct is the one from President Washington, excerpted from his final speech to the two Houses of Congress, on

143. Those who have been blessed enough to regularly visit the Jamie L. Whitten Building will tell you that address may sound good, but it won't get you to the correct door to actually enter the building. Try instead 1400 Jefferson Drive SW.

December 7, 1796: "With reference either to individual or national welfare, agriculture is of primary importance."

Notwithstanding the comparative length of the chiseled quotes from Saint Paul and President Lincoln, President Washington's quote is cut short. Immediately after the line chiseled on the Whitten Building, the next line of his speech reads, "In proportion as nations advance in population, and other circumstances of maturity, this truth becomes more apparent, and renders the cultivation of the soil more and more an object of public patronage."[144] In context, Washington was calling for the founding of a national agricultural society, which did not come into being for another ten or so years.[145]

Washington's larger point was that agriculture would grow even more important as the United States grew. He believed that this truth would become more apparent as society expanded and the economy diversified. Most farmers would tell you that Washington was certainly right about the enduring importance of the agriculture industry. They would likely dicker, however, with his prediction that the elected officials of our day believe this truth has become more apparent. Most farm and ag sector leaders would tell you they feel more and more invisible. At a minimum, they would tell you that their work to educate and influence elected officials has gotten harder.

History is littered with politicians who have said nice things about farmers. My favorite is from Williams Jennings Bryan. Bryan, a member of the Democratic Party, ran for president in 1896 and lost. He maintained control of the Democratic Party and clinched

---

144. United States Department of Agriculture, Report of the Commissioner of Patents (United States: USDA, 1860), Google Books. *https://books.google.com/books?id=lz87AQAAMAAJ&pg=PA22&lpg=PA22&dq=%22with+reference+ to+either+individual+or+national%22&source= bl&ots=tv9nBhU8nw&sig=ACfU3U0safrbeMXsHBvWYRPNuH_69jKqcw&hl=en&sa=X&ved=2ahUKEwizgcGwlunyAhX2FlkFHW2zAf0Q6AF6BAgIEAM#v=onepage&q=%22with%20reference%20to%20either%20individual%20or%20national%22&f=false.*

145. And when it was borne, in Georgetown, it was called the "Columbian Agricultural Society for the promotion of Rural and Domestic Economy." This was obviously before those occupying the nation's capital city perfected the art of the acronym.

the nomination again in 1900. When he lost a second time. He also lost in 1908. But Woodrow Wilson was kind enough to make him the Secretary of State in 1913. Secretary Bryan also had a daughter named Ruth Baird Bryan Leavitt Owen Rohde. He had two other children, but as far as I can tell none of them ended up with six names. Which is sort of a letdown.

Perhaps more known for his barnstorming political speeches than his political consulting on how to narrowly avoid the White House, Bryan delivered his most famous tribute to agriculture during the 1896 Democratic convention, in the context of a national debate about the country's monetary policy:

> *You come to us and tell us that the great cities are in favor of the gold standard; we reply that the great cities rest upon our broad and fertile prairies. Burn down your cities and leave our farms, and your cities will spring up again as if by magic; but destroy our farms, and the grass will grow in the streets of every city in the country.*

I have spoken to hundreds of ag audiences over the years, and reciting Bryan's quote from memory always evokes agreeable eyes and nodding heads. Bryan is not alone, however, in his effusive praise for the men and women of the plow. Going back further, the words of Thomas Jefferson come to mind:

> *Cultivators of the earth are the most valuable citizens. They are the most vigorous, the most independent, the most virtuous, and they are tied to their country*

> *and wedded to its liberty and interests by the most lasting bands.*[146]

Jefferson penned these words in a 1785 letter to John Jay, a fellow Founding Father and the first chief justice of the U.S. Supreme Court.

The homage paid by key elected leaders in the days of yore might have had more to do with raw politics than authentic respect for the industry. The first commissioner of agriculture under Lincoln, who we would today refer to as the United States Secretary of Agriculture,[147] was a man named Isaac Newton. This is confusing. The agriculturalist Isaac Newton was not the same person as the English physicist of the same name, who was born in 1643. Sir Isaac Newton would have been 219 years old by the time Lincoln appointed the earlier Isaac Newton to run the Department of Agriculture.

Speaking of the key role farmers played in society at the time, Newton reflected in 1863:

> *He has a sturdy independence of character, adorned, perhaps by culture and refinement. He belongs to a class of citizens who hold in their hands five-sixths of the wealth of the country and its entire political power; and the hands which have wrought this wealth are able to defend the Constitution which makes us one people.*[148]

---

146. Some versions of this quote end with the word "bonds" as opposed to "bands." I have chosen to quote from the Jefferson Quotes & Family Letters website. "Extract from Thomas Jefferson to John Jay," Jefferson Quotes, The Jefferson Monticello, last modified __, 2021, *https://tjrs.monticello.org/letter/69.*

147. In 1885, Norman Jay Coleman, to whom New York, Kentucky, Indiana, and Missouri can all lay claim, became the United States Commissioner of Agriculture. He was appointed by President Grover Cleveland. In February of 1889, he became the first Secretary of the Department of Agriculture, a role he filled for fewer than thirty days.

148. Report of the Commissioner of Agriculture for the Year 1862, January 1, 1863. Available at: *https://www.jlindquist.com/newton.html.*

Your author has not tried to verify the wealth or political clout Newton attributes to the 1860s farmer class here. My fear is that Newton's approximation might be slightly exaggerated, and on this one I would like to remain blissfully ignorant.

TIMES, THEY ARE A-CHANGING

What is unmistakable, though, is that even if farmers once held Newton's estimation of 83.33 percent of the economic prowess and 100 percent of the political power in the United States 160 years ago, they don't anymore.

In the 2020 presidential primary, Michael Bloomberg was rightly roasted for remarks he made at a 2016 appearance at the University of Oxford in England. While addressing students at the Said Business School, he blithely maintained, "I could teach anybody—even people in this room so no offense intended—to be a farmer. It's a process. You dig a hole, you put a seed in, you put dirt on top, add water, up comes the corn." It seems the mayor thought the countryside was one big Chia Pet. Farm leaders and commentators alike have enjoyed publicly correcting Bloomberg, a task not necessary here.[149]

Fortunately, Bloomberg's comments do not reflect the views of most of our elected officials. Indeed, he later explained that they didn't even adequately reflect his own views. The elected officials I have been blessed to work with over the years generally respect the hard work of America's farmers and want to be supportive of their contributions to our economy and society. Even during the Obama years, which corresponded closely to the height of the Michael Pollan–inspired food movement, no public official blatantly insulted farmers or expressed outright animosity toward them.

149. Victor Davis Hanson, "The Farming Wit and Wisdom of Mike Bloomberg," *The National Review*, February 18, 2020, *https://www.nationalreview.com/corner/the-farming-wit-and-wisdom-of-mike-bloomberg/*.

Even so, those who represent agriculture in the political forums of our day will tell you that their jobs are getting harder. The skepticism of "big ag," "corporate farming," and "industrial agriculture" is palatable among the twentysomethings that populate Congressional offices and staff the political operations of Cabinet agencies. One seasoned D.C. lobbyist who regularly represents agricultural clients before the House, Senate, and the administration shared with me that, during his career, he has seen a palpable shift among the staffers who cover the agriculture portfolio. For years, the predominant resume among ag staffers was that they had grown up on farms. They had a familial interest in agricultural policy. They knew producers and had been around enough of them to anticipate their point of view and what their reactions would be to ag policy proposals. As of late, the agriculture lobbyist and his colleagues run into those who learned all they need to know about agriculture on social media. The new generation of staffers is more prone to ask, incredulous toward any pushback, "Why can't we do it this way?" One group is growing in numbers while the other wanes. It's not hard to guess which is which.

There are some food system outsiders that would flatly disagree with my premise. In other words, some key outsider voices believe the ag community has a firm grip on Washington, and that it is all too effective at thwarting needed reforms. In an October 2016 *New York Times* piece, Michael Pollan credits the ag industry's strong lobby for the lack of more "progress," and basically excuses the Obamas' failure to "take on corporate agriculture" while they were the farmers-in-chief.[150] Pollan observed that the food movement he had championed in the first few years of this millennium was quashed by the big food and big meat lobbyists. He concluded in

150. It never crosses Pollan's mind that much of the vapid noise around transforming the food system is difficult to translate into policy once individuals who earn a living growing and selling food have an opportunity to explain the justifications for their actions to lawmakers and leaders.

2016 that "the food movement still barely exists as a political force in Washington." Perhaps Pollan just should have been more patient.

In a 2019 piece entitled "The End of Big Food," Helena Bottemiller Evich wrote about the splintering of the Grocery Manufacturers Association, which gave rise to the "horrible meeting" that I recounted in Chapter 1. In her Politico article, Evich begins, "The era of 'big food' is over in Washington."[151] The article mostly addresses the great divorce within the food-manufacturing community itself, explaining that it is difficult for an association to reflect the wide array of views of an industry that has so many competing perspectives. An anonymous source is quoted as saying, "This is the new norm . . . It's not just the fact that there was a lack of consensus within GMA, or that they made mistakes; it's the state of the industry. Food in general is just changing."

Just as food and food lobbying is changing, so is farming. Note the parallel between the splintering of the food lobby and what could be, in coming years, the bifurcation of the farming lobby. I can see it now. The old guard and the new guard. You can guess which one will style themselves as the good guys.

The political debate on food has obviously never been about whether food is a good thing to have, or whether food should be banned. Instead, the call to action was always about transitioning the food system to a "good food," "slow food," or "small food" enterprise. Similarly, much to Larry Kudlow's chagrin, the more recent debates about the level of funding funneled to farming have not really been about whether federal subsidies and price supports should exist. Instead, the criticism mainly reflects views on which farmers should be entitled to the help. It is a modern-day miracle

151. Helena Bottemiller Evich, "The end of Big Food," *Politico,* October 10, 2019, *https://www.politico.com/news/2019/10/10/food-industry-consumer-brands-association-043892.*

that aggies don't root one another away from the trough more than they presently do.[152]

THE DEBATES AT HAND

A recent report released by U.S. Senate Agriculture Committee (at the time) Ranking Member Debbie Stabenow (now Chair) analyzes President Trump's unprecedented Market Facilitation Program payments, which your author may know a thing or two about. Senator Stabenow's observation was that these payments were "benefitting wealthy farms and foreign companies instead of small farms."[153] Read carefully, the well-staffed and adept senator is not actually saying that the administration and Congress should turn the spigot off. Instead, the admonition is that the elected class just needs to be more careful about who gets to put their bucket underneath it. At least in the modern era, Washington has never been serious about curbing spending or subsidies. The most vigorous debate is more parochial: Which one of our constituencies should get the loot?

Admittedly, Stabenow was on to something: 2021 ended a three-year period with more federal government support for farmers than in any similar span in U.S. history. While trade assistance payments may have wound down, a June 15, 2021, USDA press release indicates the C-130s full of cash are still rumbling down the runway, headed for the heartland. The fine folks at the Farm Service Agency are dutifully shoving it out of the cargo hold as quickly as they can: "Since January, USDA has allocated $11B to producers

---

152. At the risk of offending my friends, the game of chess played by industry insiders who maneuver for their parts of the Farm Bill Title I pie is a spectacle unmatched in ag economic significance.

153. U.S. Senate Committee on Agriculture, Nutrition, and Forestry, "Minority Staff Report" (United States: Market Facilitation Program Report, 2019), U.S. Senate Committee on Agriculture, Nutrition, and Forestry, available at: *https://www.agriculture.senate.gov/imo/media/doc/MFP%20Report%20FINAL.pdf.*

and food and ag business."[154] Another $350 million in dairy assistance was announced in August 2021, albeit from the site of an idyllic Vermont dairy, and not one of the larger ones farther west that supply more dairy to more people. Turns out that pandemic assistance has replaced trade assistance. We can all await the Ag Committee's analysis.

I'm fond of saying that one of the primary determinants of agricultural success in the U.S. is government policy. Trade payments. Pandemic assistance. Farm Bill payments. Conservation funding. Crop insurance. The reach and value of each of these is determined in Washington. Let's face it. Elected officials pick winners and losers, instill mandates and decide when to waive them, dictate many of our international marketing opportunities, drive our health care and education costs, regulate what we apply and when we apply it, and are rumored to have a thing or two to say about what energy we develop, deploy, and consume. For those who want to debate the waxing or waning of the "era of big government," they might want to speak with an agribusiness owner first. The people who are "here to help" are everywhere. Some of them even carry checkbooks, even more near and dear to the heart of American farmers than President Obama's famous phone and pen.

So who is making the decisions? With agriculture and agribusiness being a top five industry in over half of our states, surely we are well represented in Congress? Well, it depends on whom you ask. I can argue it either way.

---

154. Farm Service Agency, "USDA Announces Additional Aid to Ag Producers and Businesses in Pandemic Assistance for Producers Initiative," U.S. Department of Agriculture, June 15, 2021, *https://www.fsa.usda.gov/news-room/news-releases/2021/usda-announces-additional-aid-to-ag-producers-and-businesses-in-pandemic-assistance-for-producers-initiative.*

FARMERS ON THE HILL

In 2021, the Congressional Research Service updated its biennial report profiling the membership of the current Congress.[155] Not surprisingly, the report points out that "the dominant professions of [congressional members] are public service/politics, business, and law." I was surprised to see CRS report there are 27 farmers, ranchers, or cattle farm owners in Congress (6 in the Senate, 21 in the House). With slots for 435 House members and 100 Senators, it appears that, as a percentage, farm owners make up about 5 percent of the overall elected officials class in Washington, D.C.

Another way to count farmer noses on the Hill is to check the USDA subsidy database. In October of 2020, the Environmental Working Group reported that 33 members of Congress and their immediate family members collected farm subsidies between 1995 and 2020.[156] This is in no way an endorsement of EWG's data, but those numbers appear to corroborate the CRS data (albeit that EWG number is cumulative, not a snapshot).

One could look at the data and argue that farmers are overrepresented in Congress. They make up about 5 percent of the membership but constitute only slightly more than 1 percent of the total U.S. population. But before you crow about that, you should know that 5 percent figure marks a steep decline in farmer representation since the end of World War II.

A progressive-leaning think tank called the Brookings Institution and a conservative-leaning one called the American Enterprise

155. Congressional Research Service, *Membership of the 117th Congress: A Profile* (United States: CRS Report, 2021), Congressional Research Service. *https://crsreports.congress.gov/product/pdf/R/R46705#:~:text=47%20Senators%20with%20previous%20House,in%20the%20House%2C%20plus%205.*

156. Jared Hayes, "Members of Congress Got Nearly $16 Million in Farm Subsidies and Trade War Bailout," *Environmental Working Group,* October 8, 2020, *https://www.ewg.org/news-insights/news/members-congress-got-nearly-16-million-farm-subsidies-and-trade-war-bailout#:~:text=News%20%26%20Insights-,Members%20of%20Congress%20Got%20Nearly%20%2416%20Million%20in%20Farm%20Subsidies,from%20EWG%27s%20Farm%20Subsidy%20Database.*

Institute jointly publish a document entitled "Vital Statistics on Congress," which has tracked the professions of Congressional members over the past 70 years.[157] In 1953, the House had 63 members whose occupation before being sworn into the Congress was agriculture, while the Senate had 21. Converting the numbers for that Congress to a percentage, it was over 15 percent agrarian. Again, it is now down to about 5 percent. The clearest trendline here is that farmer participation in the Congress is in decline, even if we are still "holding our own." That both the country as a whole and the country's representative democracy employs fewer farmers than it did fifty years ago is really no surprise. Equally unsurprising were the results of the 2020 Census, which tracked the continuing decline of rural political horsepower.

The shrinking number of aggies working under the dome has been felt in ways other than just what shows up in the raw data. A prominent agriculture lobbyist told me in 2021 that the House Agriculture Committee had to actively recruit members to join the Committee. For the first time in history, the aggie bus in the U.S. House had empty seats. There are 47 slots to fill on the House committee alone, so even if all the farmers in the chamber joined it, they'd have to recruit over two dozen more. This turned out to be quite a challenge in 2021.

In the Senate, members still mostly appear to jockey feverishly to join the Committee, which is why there were some raised eyebrows when the Committee welcomed its first vegan in January of 2021.[158] In the administrative agencies, it is increasingly difficult

157. Brookings, "Vital Statistics on Congress," *Brookings,* February 8, 2021, *https://www.brookings.edu/multi-chapter-report/vital-statistics-on-congress/.*

158. I remember standing in my backyard in December of 2014 when Senator Tillis called me on a Saturday to discuss the phone call he had just received from Senate Majority Leader Mitch McConnell. He explained that he had been assigned to both the Agriculture Committee and to Judiciary. My heart soared, even if I was in disbelief. To this day, my close friends Chris, Joe, Kasey, Mary, and Sarah still mock my Southern accent with: "He got Ag and Judiciary!" I ended up as the lead staffer on both. Which was one of many mistakes I made in Washington.

to find staffers who are from farming families or who are willing to give agricultural groups the same airtime they would give the food police. I spoke to one respected ag association leader who had sought a meeting with a key figure at USDA from January of 2021 to November of that same year, and who had not yet been afforded an audience. And that was at USDA. Can you imagine the hold time at FDA?

THINK TANKS THINKING ABOUT AG

It is not just the numbers that should be concerning. It is worth mentioning that there are entities that have dedicated staff that work hard to oppose farm programs and much of the ag industry-sponsored ag policy effort. Washington "think" tanks (which should absolutely never, ever be confused with "do" tanks) on the right and the left offer one proposal after another in the agriculture space. Neither political side has a monopoly on good ideas, and think tanks with roots on either side of the aisle often make recommendations based on misunderstandings of how farming actually works or which simply repeat bumper sticker slogans. Their solutions are often unworkable, would require political suicide to implement, and ignore the carefully negotiated lines of committee jurisdiction that are guarded ferociously by chairs and their staff directors. While they generally are no match for the farm and food lobbies, they nonetheless do require time and energy to oppose, and are often greeted approvingly by classical liberals and budget-conscious social conservatives.

A more qualitative assessment of the agriculture industry's clout in Washington can be drawn from the modern-day kerfuffle that was the writing of the 2018 Farm Bill.

A CASE STUDY IN AG'S MODERN-DAY CLOUT

Farm Bills are not easy. The first one is still the most famous, the Agricultural Adjustment Act of 1933. It was a part of newly minted President Franklin D. Roosevelt's New Deal programs. The act bribed farmers into limiting production across seven key commodities, with the ultimate hope that lower production levels would raise the market value and provide farmers with a return much closer to what economists at the time called "parity." A deep, historical dive into the workings of the original Farm Bill makes for interesting reading, but is only relevant here because such research would immediately reveal that even the first Farm Bill faced a near-death experience.

In fact, in January of 1936, the U.S. Supreme Court struck the first Farm Bill down as unconstitutional, both because the court took issue with the fact that the subsidies for the farmers were recovered from agricultural processors (an illegal tax), and because it believed federal legislation of this nature violated the Tenth Amendment.[159] Don't miss that. In 1936, the U.S. Supreme Court concluded that the regulation of farming by the federal government was unconstitutional. In the Court's view, such regulation was a power delegated to (or reserved by) the states exclusively. Associate Justice Owen Josephus Roberts wrote: "The [A]ct invades the reserved rights of the states. It is a statutory plan to regulate agricultural production, a matter beyond the powers delegated to the federal government."

Interestingly, this was one of the last cases in which the Four Horsemen on the U.S. Supreme Court were joined by Justice Roberts to strike down a New Deal program. At the end of that same year, FDR completely trounced Republican Kansas Governor Alf Landon in the 1936 presidential election. Landon won 8 electoral college votes to FDR's 523.[160] As a result, the President enjoyed wide

159. *United States v. Butler*, 297 U.S. 1 (1936).

160. Landon carried Vermont and Maine. I am as dumbfounded as you are by this.

majorities in both bodies of Congress, palatable public support, and a determination to see his programs survive the 5–4 conservative Supreme Court's analysis.

Shortly after Roosevelt revealed his court-packing plan, which would have allowed him to appoint an additional justice for every justice on the Court who was over the age of seventy, Justice Roberts (who had written the decision striking down the first Farm Bill) found new religion. He suddenly found less to be concerned about when analyzing the constitutionality of the breadth of Roosevelt's programs (including an upstart program called Social Security). Roberts's waning interest in constitutional suspicion was, as every law student in America is taught in Constitutional Law class, "the switch in time that saved nine."[161]

By February of 1936, Congress had adopted a do-over of the 1933 Farm Bill, in legislation entitled the Soil Conservation and Domestic Allotment Act. This marked the birth of the connection between farm income support and the implementation of conservation measures, a practice that continues to this day.

We are now on our eighteenth Farm Bill, the most recent of which is the Agricultural Improvement Act of 2018. A bound copy sits atop my piano, rarely disturbed. One of only three known fully executed "red lines" of the bill is safely ensconced in a frame that sits on my bonus room floor, too precious to hang.[162] It is signed by Speaker of the House Paul Ryan, acting President pro tempore of the Senate John Boozman, President Donald Trump, and Secretary of Agriculture Sonny Perdue.[163] Getting to the "all smiles" signing ceremony held at

161. All that said, *Butler* has never been expressly overturned by the Supreme Court.

162. A "red line" is Washington-speak for an original, signed copy of an enrolled bill, or at least the first and last pages of such a bill, which has by its enactment become a public law. It is also the name of one of the routes of the Metro, which by the way will not get you to the Capitol and is probably late or under renovation.

163. This was a gift given to me by my colleagues at USDA upon my escape from the Capital beltline in late spring 2019. I hold it dear, but not nearly as dear as I do the friendships—and thousands of hours of staff time—it represents.

the White House in December of 2018 was, however, anything but a cakewalk.[164]

A little history will set the stage. Prior to 1973, the Farm Bill was not the shotgun wedding between farm programs and food stamps that it is today. Senator Bob Dole, from Kansas, correctly reasoned back then that he could increase the likelihood of passing the Farm Bill if it contained something for both rural, more agrarian-minded members of Congress and their more urban counterparts. This gave birth to the arranged marriage between the food stamps part of the federal government's food assistance program and the federal government's typical five-year-cycle farm-aid package. The matrimony has lasted since then, but as recent Farm Bill cycles have revealed, significant counseling has been required to avoid a divorce.

Fast forward to 2018. The Republican-controlled House of Representatives, in their version of the Farm Bill, included a number of reforms to the Supplemental Food Assistance Program (SNAP, the modern-day food stamp program). One of the more modest of these proposals was that able-bodied, working-age adults without dependents (known as ABAWDs in Washington) should work or at least try to find work if they were to remain eligible for the program for longer than three months.[165] To be even more clear, if an individual was outside of the legal working age parameters (18–49), was

164. The 2013 Farm Bill was no less of a train wreck. It had to be reincarnated several times, not the least of which was its very public obliteration on the House floor because of an amendment offered by Representative Steve Southerland, a Republican from Florida, that would have allowed states to stiffen work requirements for SNAP recipients. The bill was creeping toward floor passage when Representative Southerland offered his amendment, which passed by a vote of 227 to 198. Only thirty-two minutes later, the Federal Agriculture Reform and Risk Management Act went down 234 to 195. Don't worry. The legislation was resuscitated and eventually signed into law by President Obama on the eve of Valentine's Day 2014. By then, love was clearly in the air.

165. U.S. Department of Agriculture, *Supplemental Nutrition Assistance Program: Requirements for Able-Bodied Adults without Dependents* (United States: Food and Nutrition Service, 2018) U.S. Department of Agriculture, *available at: https://fns-prod.azureedge.net/sites/default/files/snap/ABAWDtoOFR.pdf.*

unfit for work, had a dependent child, or was pregnant, they were already exempt from the looking-for-work requirement.

Existing law allowed for states to apply to USDA for a waiver of this provision, and by 2018, the creativity of the laboratories of democracy across the U.S. in seeking to take advantage of such USDA-issued waivers was on full display. One of the more common approaches used by states to increase SNAP access was to combine counties with lower unemployment rates and counties with higher unemployment rates into one geographic waiver area request. In this way, the work or search for work requirement for able-bodied, working age adults without dependents could be waived for a broader geographic community of (more) SNAP applicants.[166]

The House, led by Texas Representative and House Agriculture Committee Chairman Mike Conaway intended to tighten down on this practice. Their version of the Farm Bill did just that, but when it reached the floor the first time, it failed by a vote of 198–213.[167] A group of thirty House Republicans—the House Freedom Caucus—doomed it. But not because of the reforms to the SNAP program. They voted against the bill on the floor in May of 2018 because they were not given assurances that they would have the opportunity to consider a completely unrelated bill involving immigration first. Chairman Conaway and his staff worked adroitly to keep the bill on

166. Just to prove just how complicated the ABAWDs issue can be, Senator and Presidential hopeful Kirsten Gillibrand questioned Secretary Perdue about the Department's efforts to tighten the loopholes referenced here in a Senate hearing in February of 2019. Secretary Perdue took pains to explain that the rule USDA had proposed applied only to "adults able to work," although the Senator never seemed to relent on her point that the Department should have done an analysis to determine whether making adults who are able to work return to work to remain eligible for the program might negatively impact them. United States Senate Committee on Agriculture, Nutrition, & Forestry, "Implementing the Agriculture Improvement Act of 2018," Full Committee Hearing, 2:24:40, posted February 28, 2019, *https://www.agriculture.senate.gov/hearings/implementing-the-agriculture-improvement-act-of-2018.*

167. Congressional Research Service, *Farm Bills: Major Legislative Actions, 1965-2018* (United States: CRS Report, 2018), Congressional Research Service, available at: *https://sgp.fas.org/crs/misc/R45210.pdf.*

life support until it eventually passed the House by a vote of 213–211 on June 21, 2018.

Pause here for a moment to consider what happened to the Farm Bill in May and June of 2018. Republicans in the House made reforms to the domestic food aid parts of the Farm Bill, but a group of thirty Republicans nonetheless voted against the Farm Bill to extract a promise from House leadership for action on another piece of legislation. They were willing to risk passage of the most important, most seminal piece of ag legislation considered by Congress every five years because they had other priorities they wanted to pursue. This does not sound like a Congress beholden to agriculture's political clout as described by Commissioner Isaac Newton in the 1860s.

The Senate had, in the meantime, been moving their own version of the Farm Bill. It was no secret that they held little admiration for the House-approved ABAWD reform. For that matter, they had little admiration for many of the other House food aid program reforms. Without a filibuster-proof caucus, Senate Ag Committee Chairman Pat Roberts simply did not have the heft to move the bill across the finish line without the agreement of Senate Ag Committee Ranking Member Debbie Stabenow. On their bill, the two Senators garnered an impressive bipartisan vote of 20–1 in committee, and on June 28, 2018, passed their bill by a vote of 86–11 on the Senate floor.

What happened next was predictable. Nothing. That is, until the Republicans lost the House in the November 2018 elections. They then realized there was no viable path for legislatively enacting their SNAP reforms and agreed to look to USDA to use its rulemaking authority to address some of the abuses they identified in the ABAWD work-requirement waiver process. It was the USDA's rulemaking promise that kept Republicans and President Trump (and his able

OMB staff) at the table for passage of the final conference report.[168] Absent these circumstances, no amount of agricultural-community consternation would have resolved the stalemate. Now you see why more and more ag policy watchers are questioning the wisdom of asking SNAP advocates and farm program proponents to continually renew their Farm Bill marital vows.

In the words of Ken Barbic, assistant Secretary for Congressional Relations at USDA during the Perdue administration, "Fewer and fewer Democrats feel political pressure to deliver on farm programs and fewer Republicans are supportive of food aid programs that lack meaningful guardrails." In fact, even the Republican caucus is more and more skeptical of farm programs, not to mention some, ahem, recent Republican presidents, or at least their demigod OMB appointees.

Barbic had a front-row seat for the 2018 Farm Bill negotiations. He observed that today's red state/blue state phenomenon has, in the absence of any sizable Democratic blue dog caucus (or any other discernable "middle"), left the ag constituency in a treacherous place. According to Barbic, "Whether or not the Republicans take the House in 2022, the loss of Collin Peterson on the Democratic side leaves a hole that cannot be easily filled in the 2023 Farm Bill debate. Gaining his seat helps Republicans take back the House, but passing bipartisan legislation will be even more difficult than in 2018."

---

168. I still remember the late night, early-December 2018 phone conversation that Ken Barbic and I had with Shahira Knight, the President's top Capitol Hill liaison and all-around genius, explaining that we hoped this "let's use rulemaking, which the Farm Bill did nothing to forestall" strategy would be enough to help avoid a situation in which far-right House members somehow talked President Trump into vetoing the Farm Bill. It worked.

AG'S ISSUES OUTSIDE OF THE FARM BILL AND OUTSIDE OF WASHINGTON

The winnowing clout of the farm community can also be seen outside the Farm Bill debate. In March of 2021, U.S. House members Zoe Lofgren (D-CA), and Dan Newhouse (R-WA) introduced H.R. 1603, entitled the "Farm Workforce Modernization Act of 2021."[169] The legislation ultimately passed the House on March 18, 2021. While the American Farm Bureau and a number of state Farm Bureau federations appreciated the attention to the agriculture community's labor needs, they generally opposed the bill in the form in which it passed the House. In fact, American Farm Bureau whipped against a vote on the bill at all. They lost. To rephrase: an ag labor bill passed the House over the objections of the nation's largest farm organization.

The decline is not limited to Washington. California recently adopted a ballot initiative that will decimate any remaining pork industry there, and unless the U.S. Supreme Court takes action will rewrite how pork is produced in some of its neighboring states. Ag groups opposed it and worked to prevent its adoption. They lost. In Maine, voters just approved a state constitutional amendment that declares that all people have a "natural, inherent, and unalienable right" to grow and consume food. The Farm Bureau there opposed the amendment, mostly because of concerns that nobody knows what it means. It passed anyway.

The point here is that much is said of "big agriculture" and its grip on Washington and elsewhere. And farmers have, in recent history, often punched above their weight—ethanol and biofuels policy is a good example of their success. But the forecast is not promising. With aggies making up a smaller and smaller portion of the

169. According to the Congressional Budget Office, H.R. 1603 "would allow unlawfully present aliens (non-U.S. nationals) who are working in agriculture to receive Certified Agricultural Worker Status (CAWS) and, eventually, lawful permanent resident (LPR) status. Using data from the Department of Agriculture, Department of Labor, and DHS, CBO estimates that more than 300,000 workers and 200,000 of their dependents would receive CAWS."

American electorate, a similar fate likely awaits their participation percentage in elected office. It most assuredly awaits their win-loss record on actual legislation and administrative action.

Imagine if the Fair Labor Standards Act was passed for the first time today. Would farm groups and ag-friendly legislators be able to obtain agriculture exemptions from the minimum wage and overtime?[170]

Need another example that doesn't require your imagination?

OSHA was created in 1971. Five years later, Congress began attaching a rider to the agency's budget that exempted farms with ten or fewer employees from certain OSHA investigations and enforcement.[171] In 2020, that rider came shockingly close to not being included in the final appropriations package.

Heaven forbid we take a look at the ag community's abject failure to navigate a successful path of resolution on the foreign workforce issues that are so critical for the sector's future. I won't write about this here, but not because of space constraints. It's because of what reflecting on twenty years of "maybe we can make some progress next year" does to my blood pressure. It seems that the level of attention and work on this particular issue is consistently on the rise, but progress on any real solution stays wistfully just out of reach.

The political forum is just one more place where farmers' power seems to be slipping away. Concomitantly, agriculture and food system outsiders' influence over farm policy appears to be gaining ground. If the Farmers v. Foodies World Series were hosted in Washington, I'm not sure it would take all seven games to crown a champion.

---

170. United States Department of Labor, *Fact Sheet #12: Agricultural Employers Under the Fair Labor Standards Act (FLSA)* (United States: Wage and Hour Division, 2020), U.S. Department of Labor. *https://www.dol.gov/sites/dolgov/files/WHD/legacy/files/whdfs12.pdf.*

171. United States Department of Labor, *Farming Appropriations Rider* (United States: OSHA, 1992), U.S. Department of Labor. *https://www.osha.gov/laws-regs/standardinterpretations/1992-07-22.*

Oh yeah. Those other two quotes on the Whitten Building. Lincoln's reads:

> *No other human occupation opens so wide a field for the profitable and agreeable combination of labor with cultivated thought as agriculture.*

And Saint Paul?

> *The husbandman that laboreth must be the first partaker of the fruits.*[172]

That is, until someone passes legislation that says otherwise.

172. 2 Timothy 2:6 (Authorized King James Version). Of course we couldn't quote the ERV on a United States federal government building!

CHAPTER EIGHT

MEET ME AT THE COURTHOUSE

"The Public Justice Food Project uses strategically targeted litigation, coupled with basebuilding and storytelling, to address the structural and institutional inequities upon which our current food system is built and work toward a food system that is free from extraction and exploitation."[173]

There is a lot there.

Let's start with the basics. Public Justice is a 501(c)(3) non-profit based in Washington, D.C. According to their website, they pursue "high impact lawsuits to combat social and economic injustice, protect the Earth's sustainability, and challenge predatory corporate

173. "A Better Food System," Food Project, Public Justice, last modified November 22, 2021, *https://food.publicjustice.net/*.

conduct and government abuses."[174] In 2019, the entity reported around $6 million in revenue and sits on a nest egg of more than $10 million. A key area of focus for the organization is the modernized American food and agriculture system. The Public Justice Food Project focuses squarely on that enterprise. According to a jobs announcement posted in September of 2021: "The Food Project at Public Justice works to dismantle the current corporate-controlled exploitative food system and support a movement to achieve our vision of a food system that is both regenerative and equitable."[175]

Note the lack of subtlety. There are structural and institutional inequities within the current food system. There is also extraction and exploitation. I suspect many farmers would agree. Just not in the way Public Justice means it. They are about the business of dismantling. They are supporting a movement. They have a vision of what the agricultural system should look like. And a big part of their plan for achieving that vision calls for lawyers, aggrieved parties, litigation, and courtrooms. And they are not alone.

The Lewis & Clark Law School is home to the Center for Animal Law Studies and the most extensive animal law curriculum in the world. Law students can take one or several of more than twenty-five diverse animal law courses, with eighteen distinct courses in rotation each year. The Law School also bestows the only advanced legal degree—a Master's of Legal Letters—in Animal Law. "The Animal Law LLM Program is designed for U.S. and international law school graduates who wish to focus on animal law in practice, teaching, research, or public policy."[176]

---

174. "About and Financial Information," Who We Are, Public Justice, last modified November 22, 2021, *https://www.publicjustice.net/who-we-are/mission/*.

175. Public Justice, *Food Project Staff Attorney* (D.C.: Public Justice, 2021), Public Justice Upload, available at *https://www.publicjustice.net/wp-content/uploads/2021/09/2021.09.16-RE-POST-of-Food-Project-Staff-Attorney-Announcement.pdf*.

176. "About Us," About CALS, Lewis & Clark, last modified March 29, 2021, *https://law.lclark.edu/centers/animal_law_studies/about_us/*.

There's nothing wrong with studying animal law. Like any other field, the legal protections regarding animals, and the standards required of their owners, can be complicated. The American Pet Products Association recently reported that pet ownership in the U.S. rose to an all-time high of 70 percent in 2020.[177] With seven in ten U.S. households owning a pet, some legal issues will inevitably arise. Liability. Leashing. The untimely death of an animal. And even veterinarian malpractice and estate planning. Many of us consider our pets to be members of our family.

Most relevant here, the Lewis & Clark version of animal law extends to livestock. In 2019, the Law School launched the Animal Law Litigation Clinic (ALLC), which they refer to as "the world's first and only legal clinic devoted to advancing legal protections for farmed animals."[178] It is unclear precisely which animals count as "farmed," but the website does contain photos of some really cute pigs.

In their own words, "The ALLC advocates for farmed animals in the courtroom by providing litigation support for cutting-edge lawsuits aimed at establishing and expanding legal protections and rights for farmed animals, including challenging the presumption that common, inhumane farming practices are shielded from judicial scrutiny, and pursuing novel causes of action."[179] One client of the ALLC spoke effusively of the clinic's assistance, stating that it had been able to "bring multiple, high-profile lawsuits that seek to enact meaningful change for millions of animals suffering in factory farms and industrial slaughterhouses."[180]

177. Debbie Phillips-Donaldson, "New US pet ownership study confirms pandemic-led growth," *Pet Food Industry,* June 1, 2021, *https://www.petfoodindustry.com/articles/10325-new-us-pet-ownership-study-confirms-pandemic-led-growth.*

178. "Animal Law Litigation Clinic," Animal Law Clinics, Lewis & Clark, last modified March 29, 2021, *https://law.lclark.edu/centers/animal_law_studies/animal_law_clinics/animal-law-litigation-clinic/.*

179. *Ibid.*

180. *Ibid.*

That client is not the only legal actor who believes millions of animals are suffering in factory farms and industrial slaughterhouses. Farm Sanctuary's mission is to "pursue bold solutions to end animal agriculture and foster just and compassionate vegan living."[181] I mention them here not because they advocate for a meatless society. To each his own.[182] The point here is that they are increasingly using litigation that handicaps the food system to get there. It is not enough for them to be meatless. They want all of us to be meatless. And one of their bold solutions is to sue to effectuate those ends.

When USDA's Food Safety and Inspection Service adopted a rule to allow for an optional new inspection system for market hog-slaughter establishments—a system that had been demonstrated to provide public health protection at least equivalent to the existing inspection system—Farm Sanctuary stepped in to shut it down by filing a lawsuit in federal court.[183] They saw the rule as advantageous to meat processors. They then sought a judge to stop it.

In my home state, the North Carolina Farmed Animal Save[184] is part of the "global save movement." Their mission is to shine a light on the "dark, hidden secrets of the animal agriculture industry," and they advocate to end factory farming.[185] They are also a party to the suit against the USDA, and alleged that their standing to bring

---

181. "About Us," Who We Are, Farm Sanctuary, last modified September 30, 2021, *https://www.farmsanctuary.org/about-us/.*

182. They also manage the Founding Farm Animal Sanctuary in the U.S., which has "rescued and provided refuge for countless survivors of the animal agriculture system." They currently house roughly 1,000 rescued animals in refuges in Los Angeles and Watkins Glen, N.Y. In their words, these rescued animals are "ambassadors, representing the billions of farm animals currently in the system." And to think, we thought the turkey pardon was the only way out.

183. Lewis & Clark, *United States District Court for the Western District of New York Document 22* (New York: Lewis & Clark, 2019), Lewis & Clark Files, *https://law.lclark.edu/live/files/30373-farm-sanctuary-v-usda.*

184. That is the group's name. Not a typo.

185. "We Are North Carolina Farmed Animal Save," Home, North Carolina Farmed Animal Save, last modified January 19, 2021, *http://www.ncsave.org/.*

legal action was predicated on the fact that higher slaughter speeds would increase their "aesthetic and emotional injuries."[186]

Standing is generally a legal concept that prevents parties who are not injured by an action of another party from bringing a lawsuit. Typically, to maintain a lawsuit and not have it dismissed for a lack of standing, a plaintiff must allege some direct injury or harm and demonstrate that the court is able to redress it. Just how would line speeds inside a packing plant create or increase injuries to an animal rights organization? It turns out that the Farmed Animal Save organization regularly holds vigils for the animals entering the plants. With more animals coming in, they will have to hold more vigils. They will therefore experience greater distress. If that wasn't enough, they also alleged that their increased vigils will mean they "face a substantially increased risk of exposure to a host of environmental impacts, some of them health-threatening, at slaughterhouses, including exposure to increased air pollution, waste, and wastewater."[187]

There are others.

Animal Equity. The Animal Legal Defense Fund. The Center for Biological Diversity. Mercy for Animals. Animal Outlook, previously Compassion Over Killing.[188] The Animal Welfare Institute. Iowa Citizens for Community Improvement. Food and Water Watch. Sustainable Agriculture Project. Compassion in World Farming. Farm Forward. The Environmental Justice Network. Water protectors,

---

186. Lewis & Clark, *United States District Court for the Western District of New York Document 22* (New York: Lewis & Clark, 2019), Lewis & Clark Files, *https://law.lclark.edu/live/files/30373-farm-sanctuary-v-usda.*

187. Lewis & Clark, *United States District Court for the Western District of New York Document 22* (New York: Lewis & Clark, 2019), Lewis & Clark Files, *https://law.lclark.edu/live/files/30373-farm-sanctuary-v-usda.*

188. This organization describes itself as a nonprofit, tax-exempt 501(c)(3) that works to "challenge the status quo of animal agribusiness, expose the truth, deliver justice, revolutionize food systems, and empower others to stand up for animals by leaving them off of their plates." Lewis & Clark, *United States District Court for the Western District of New York Document 13* (New York: Lewis & Clark, 2020), Lewis & Clark Files, *https://law.lclark.edu/live/files/30372-farm-sanctuary-v-perdue.*

keepers, and alliances. The Rural Empowerment Association for Community Health. One longtime thought leader in the ag space called it a "spider-web of influence and advocacy organizations." All of these entities leverage the legal system to effectuate their preferred policy outcomes.

In 2016, the Animal Legal Defense Fund sued Hormel, claiming the luncheon meat maker's advertising violated the District of Columbia's consumer protection law. ALDF argued that Hormel's advertising campaign "Make the Natural Choice" was false and misleading, and premised that criticism on the fact that Hormel sells meat from animals that are, in ALDF's words, "born, raised, and killed in unnatural, unsafe, and cruel conditions."[189] Hormel moved successfully to have the case dismissed at the trial court level, given that food labeling claims are typically preempted by federal law, but the D.C. Court of Appeals (the District's version of a state supreme court) revived the case. The appellate court found that ALDF had both standing to sue and that federal food labeling laws did not preempt ALDF's state-law based claims. This ability to use state-based consumer protection laws to sue commercial food producers even when claims they make in advertising would pass muster if they were on the package opens a new front against farmers and food manufacturers, and it is one with fifty-one different nuances. That is precisely why ALDF brought the case and styled their claims in the manner they did.

Not all the action is aimed at livestock or animal production. Earthjustice refers to itself as the premier non-profit public interest environmental law organization in the world. They claim to "wield the power of law and the strength of partnership to protect people's

189. Complaint, *Animal Legal Defense Fund v. Hormel Foods Corp.*, Case No. 2016-CA-004744B, Superior Court of the District of Columbia, Civil Division, filed June 20, 2016.

health, to preserve magnificent places and wildlife, to advance clean energy, and to combat climate change."[190]

Here's what they think of genetically modified food and a subset of that technology, genetic engineering: "Though the debate over the health effects of eating genetically modified food continues, one thing is certain. GE crops paired with their pesticide counterparts wreak havoc on the environment through: (1) increased herbicide use; (2) increase of herbicide-resistant weeds; and (3) the contamination of organic and conventional (non-GMO) crops."[191] Elsewhere they refer to the deployment of the technology as an "environmental disaster."

That's right. The same technology that the World Food Prize recognized for opening up "uncommon opportunities for shaping the future of agriculture, industry, medicine and environment protection"—in a ceremony at the State Department in which John Kerry offered his own laudatory remarks—is, to Earthjustice, an environmental disaster.[192]

And they intend to do something about it.

Notwithstanding the lack of accuracy of their impressions of the characteristics of genetic engineering, Earthjustice is busy leveraging their lawyers to slow or stop the deployment of genetically modified or genetically engineered food crops. When Dow AgroSciences sought to bring Enlist Duo to the market in the mid-2010s, Earthjustice was there to sue. Dow's product took advantage of the genetic engineering that allowed crops to be resistant to both glyphosate and 2,4-D. Earthjustice's principal argument was that EPA failed to adequately analyze the impacts of the herbicide

190. "About Us," About Earthjustice, Earthjustice, last modified November 1, 2019, *https://earthjustice.org/about*.

191. Mike Coots, "Engineering an Environmental Disaster," *Earthjustice*, June 29, 2020, *https://earthjustice.org/features/engineering-an-environmental-disaster-2*.

192. World Food Prize Foundation, "Three Biotechnology Scientists Awarded 2013 World Food Prize," *World Food Prize Foundation*, June 19, 2013, *https://www.worldfoodprize.org/index.cfm/87428/40188/three_biotechnology_scientists_awarded_2013_world_food_prize*.

compound on human health, and thus its approval violated the Federal Insecticide, Fungicide, and Rodenticide Act (FIFRA). To be sure, there were other arguments, and while your author would enjoy parsing them all, my guess is that readers would rather I not.

As is the case with much of the legal activity that has the potential to reshape agriculture, the plaintiffs in the Enlist Duo litigation did not act alone. The Center for Food Safety lent their legal expertise, along with Beyond Pesticides, the Center for Biological Diversity, the Center for Food Safety, the Environmental Working Group, the National Family Farm Coalition, and Pesticide Action Network North America. As you can tell from their names alone, most of these groups generally oppose pesticide use in agriculture, and they have learned that litigation can be used to slow the already snail's-pace EPA registration process for new pesticides, if not outright stop or even reverse it.

Another trademark of these outside groups is their tendency to sue the government that regulates the technology as opposed to the private parties that deploy it. In some instances, they rely on statutory schemes that explicitly provide third parties with a private right of action and an opportunity to do so. This practice also begs the question, though, of why they don't go directly after the inventors, since it is those inventors who are hell-bent on promoting animal cruelty, environmental degradation, or other disaster-scale activities. Why not go after them? One answer is that doing so would deprive them of the ability to make nationwide policy by forcing a federal agency to revoke, revise, or reissue its regulations. To get that result, they have to sue, and then settle, with the relevant federal agency.

The phrase "sue and settle" is not new. President Reagan's Attorney General, Edward Meese III, penned a memo to all assistant U.S. attorneys general in March of 1986 that spelled out the trouble with such tactics. They can result "in an unwarranted expansion of the powers of the judiciary—often with the consent of government parties—at the expense of the executive and legislative branches."[193] In 2017, EPA Administrator Scott Pruitt made the news when he issued a directive to end the practice at EPA.[194] The U.S. Chamber of Commerce has written extensively about the phenomenon and even catalogs numerous examples of how special-interest groups and agencies have historically deployed the sinister practice.[195] Yet thanks largely to some of the groups mentioned above, the practice is alive and well.

A technical point here: defenders of the sue-and-settle tactic would argue that they are completely entitled to influence agency activity through litigation. Maybe so. But when that litigation results in a settlement that binds a federal or state agency to create law outside the normal rulemaking process, most of the tenants of notice and rulemaking are cast aside. The sue-and-settle process lacks transparency, skirts procedural safeguards, creates unintended tension between the three branches of government and the balance of power distributed among them, and lacks the protections a truly adversarial process brings to litigation.[196] There are numerous examples of anti-agriculture groups favorably roosting on this stratagem. Your author has been unable to find a single example of the aggies using the same tactic to achieve a result favorable for themselves.

Another reason anti-agriculture litigators would prefer to make the government their adversary is that in doing so, they might find a more sympathetic defendant. If the leadership of an executive

193. U.S. Department of Justice, *Memorandum—Office of Legal Policy* (D.C.: U.S. Department of Justice, 1986), National Archives. *https://www.archives.gov/files/news/samuel-alito/accession-060-89-1/Acc060-89-1-box9-memoAyer-LSWG-1986.pdf.*

194. Scott Pruitt, "Administrator Pruitt Issues Directive to End EPA 'Sue and Settle'," *United States Environmental Protection Agency,* October 16, 2017, *https://www.epa.gov/newsreleases/administrator-pruitt-issues-directive-end-epasue-settle.*

195. "Sue and Settle: Regulating Behind Closed Doors," Regulations, United States Chamber of Commerce, last modified March 6, 2018, *https://www.uschamber.com/regulations/sue-and-settle-regulating-behind-closed-doors.*

196. *Ibid.*

branch agency disagrees with the prior leadership of the agency (a previous president's appointees) on a regulatory point, or simply is uninterested in prioritizing a defense to that previous administration's policy-turned-regulation, they will be quite temped to settle the litigation in a way that undoes the previous administration's action. Industry sometimes attempts to intervene to police this temptation, but the rules for intervention are more conservative than the rules for original standing. Thus, the special-interest parties suing the government have a low hurdle to mount to maintain their suit, while a regulated party attempting to support the government position under attack has a high bar to jump before they can become involved in the case themselves.

I've mentioned litigation brought against agriculture by animal rights groups. And by environmentalists. But nothing compares to the two of them working together, particularly when more traditional plaintiff-oriented trial lawyers are also involved.

My friend Tiffany Dowell Lashmet has carefully chronicled the litigation against hog farmers in North Carolina known colloquially as the "hog nuisance litigation."[197] Iowa State University's Center for Agricultural Law and Taxation has also published solid reviews of the litigation.[198] Tiffany is an Agricultural Law Specialist for the Texas A&M AgriLife Extension Service. She authors an award-winning agricultural law blog and a similarly accolated podcast that might have even featured yours truly a time or two. She and Jake Parker, also a friend and the general counsel for the North Carolina Farm Bureau, have helped many understand the labyrinthic nature

197. Tiffany Dowell, "Appellate Court Affirms Liability in North Carolina Nuisance Case; Smithfield Announces Settlement," *Texas A&M AgriLife Extension - Texas Agriculture Law,* December 7, 2020, *https://agrilife.org/texasaglaw/2020/12/07/appellate-court-affirms-liability-in-north-carolina-nuisance-case-smithfield-announces-settlement/.*

198. Kitt Tovar, "An Update on North Carolina Nuisance Lawsuits," *Iowa State University—Center for Agricultural Law and Taxation,* August 31, 2018, *https://www.calt.iastate.edu/article/update-north-carolina-nuisance-lawsuits.*

of how twenty-six hog farms came to be the subject of nuisance suits brought by neighbors for odors, insects, and noises, among other things. Those neighbors—nearly five hundred of them—sued the hog-production division of Smithfield, Murphy-Brown. They were represented by a Texas law firm renowned for litigation success in the asbestos realm, and North Carolina-based Wallace and Graham, a preeminent plaintiff's firm with national connections.

Significantly, the lawyers that represented the plaintiffs in the nuisance litigation did not premise their right of recovery directly on environmental damage or health concerns. Instead, they focused on the smell of hog waste and argued that it had lowered their clients' quality of life. This allowed them to make state law nuisance claims, even though their cases were brought in federal court. In every single case tried to a jury verdict, the plaintiffs won. The farmers lost. Turns out my father was right. That smell from the hog farm of my youth truly was the smell of money . . . and the trial lawyers have now sniffed it out. I remain skeptical.

In 2020, Public Justice awarded the successful hog nuisance trial team their "Trial Lawyer of the Year" award. In their words, the "litigation is a testament to the manner in which plaintiffs' lawyers can benefit society and social justice."[199] That posturing sure is a strange way to say "thank you for putting some farmers out of business and making production move elsewhere."

Amber Miller, a widely renowned agricultural lawyer with a successful practice in Lubbock, Texas, is the former president of the American Agricultural Law Association. Her observation is that many of these lawsuits have an added layer of bitterness:

199. Public Justice, "Years-Long Struggle Against Polluting Factory Farms Wins 2020 Trial Lawyer of the Year Award," *Public Justice,* August 7, 2020, *https://www.publicjustice.net/years-long-struggle-against-polluting-factory-farms-wins-2020-trial-lawyer-of-the-year-award/.*

> *Many of thc lawsuits impacting agriculture at a broad level are simply designed to punish. The "public interest" groups, who purport to be acting on behalf of a cause, or a platform, are not pleading for meaningful changes, nor are they willing to come to the table outside of the litigation setting to discuss how any type of meaningful change may be made. Rather, the very sophisticated plaintiff's bar has determined that the assets required to engage in production agriculture otherwise equal large wealth that makes it worth "going after."*

Amber makes an important point. As farmers and farms have grown in size and value, so has the size of the target on their backs. Amber also points out that farmers may be targeted even if they are doing everything right, which clearly has a silencing effect:

> *These cases are being filed to punish even the good actors. The end result is that those good actors are now hesitant—or even refusing—to speak up, to tell the great story of production agriculture, to describe the remarkable advances that have been made in terms of input efficiencies, sustainability, animal welfare, environmental stewardship, and to come to the table to engage with those "other" groups in ways that really might achieve more meaningful landmarks. This is not ok. American consumers deserve more.*

As if Amber's words aren't poignant enough, there's plenty more proof that litigation is altering the future of American agriculture. Try using your internet search feature to find out if the ubiquitous herbicide Roundup causes cancer. The short answer is, if applied in compliance with the label, "no." At least according to the EPA.[200] Same with the European Food Safety Authority.[201] But hundreds of law firms are prepared to take your case if you feel otherwise. Tens of thousands of aggrieved parties have sued. In a very few instances, a handful have been successful. Bayer, which purchased Roundup inventor and manufacturer Monsanto for around $60 billion in 2018, has generally defended each lawsuit vigorously.

Despite maintaining—and repeatedly proving—that the product is safe for its intended use, Bayer has now announced it will reformulate glyphosate-based products in the U.S. residential lawn and garden market and rely on alternative active ingredients in them by 2023.[202] Professional and agricultural markets will still be able to purchase existing formulations. Bayer maintains that the change to its residential-facing markets "is being made exclusively to manage litigation risk and not because of any safety concerns."

Don't miss that. Roundup does not cause cancer.[203] It does, however, cause lawsuits. For the time being, farmers will continue to have access to it, but for how long? The world's largest seller of seed and crop chemicals cannot withstand billions in jury verdicts, even if they (and the EPA) are right about the product's safety. At the time of writing this, multiple groups were still actively challenging the EPA's conclusion that glyphosate doesn't pose human health risks, with the 9th U.S. Circuit Court of Appeals expected to issue a ruling on the topic sometime in the first half of 2022.

---

200. "Glyphosate," Glyphosate, United States Environmental Protection Agency, last modified date unknown, *https://www.epa.gov/ingredients-used-pesticide-products/glyphosate*.

201. Dan Charles, "Safe Or Scary? The Shifting Reputation Of Glyphosate, AKA Roundup," *NPR,* May 30, 2019, *https://www.npr.org/sections/thesalt/2019/05/30/727914874/safe-or-scary-the-shifting-reputation-of-glyphosate-aka-roundup*.

202. Glyphosate Litigation Facts, "Bayer Provides Update on Path to Closure of Roundup™ Litigation," *Glyphosate Litigation Facts,* July 29, 2021, *http://www.glyphosatelitigationfacts.com/main/media-statements/bayer-provides-update-on-path-to-closure-of-roundup-litigation/*.

203. In some cases, it doesn't even kill weeds.

Most of the discussion on this topic in the investment community revolves around a central tenant: Bayer must obtain some certainty and create finality with regard to its potential liability. If Bayer were to enter a structured settlement that put the pending tens of thousands of cases to bed, who do you think will ultimately end up paying the cost? If Roundup were to stay on the market, it certainly wouldn't get any cheaper. If it goes away, competitor Corteva will hustle to fill the void with its Enlist herbicide, but going from two choices to one for weed control is not a scenario that farmers will readily applaud.[204] Finally, what would make one think a legal defeat would be a deterrent to the judicial activists, or that a victory for Bayer would quieten things down for good?

Shifting gears, consider the challenges brought against checkoff programs over the past two decades. As most readers of this book will know, checkoffs are sometimes referred to as research and promotion programs, and they promote and provide research and information for agricultural commodities generally.[205] They do not refer to particular products, brands, or producers. The term "checkoff" comes from the fact that some of these programs formerly received funding only when farmers checked a box to signify their willingness to contribute. Today, some of these programs are mandatory under federal or state law, although producer groups do generally have control over how funds are spent, so long as they are spent according to designated statutory criteria. The amount paid into the program is generally based on a per pound, per bushel, or per head basis.

Most relevant here are the renowned beef checkoff cases, and the most renowned litigant in those is the Ranchers Cattlemen Action Legal Fund United Stockgrowers of America, or R-CALF USA.

---

204. Jacob Bunge, "Roundup Ruled the Farm, Now Its Maker Has a Challenger," *The Wall Street Journal,* January 6, 2020, *http://www.glyphosatelitigationfacts.com/main/media-statements/bayer-provides-update-on-path-to-closure-of-roundup-litigation/.*

205. "Checkoff Programs—An Overview," Checkoff, The National Agricultural Law Center, last modified May 27, 2020, *https://nationalaglawcenter.org/overview/checkoff/.*

R-CALF has challenged the constitutionality of checkoff funding under First Amendment theories, among others. Their position—that the portion of the current one dollar per head assessment that is retained by state beef councils gives rise to a constitutional violation—is diametrically opposed by the National Cattlemen's Beef Association (NCBA). The NCBA has made no secret about its views that R-CALF's efforts ultimately weaken the research and promotion potential made possible by collaboratively run state and nationally checkoff programs.

The kicker? You will never believe who does the legal work for R-CALF—Public Justice.[206] I will leave it up to you to decide why an organization that states that it wants to "dismantle corporate consolidation of power in the meat industry" would offer legal services in a case designed to alter the beef checkoff program.

In the labor law context, agricultural workers have long been exempt from certain coverage under the National Labor Relations Act (NLRA). Most relevant here, the NLRA generally provides employees with the right to form and join a union, and it prohibits any interference in this right by an employer. What the farming community may not know, however, is that there are two reasons why, in many states, this may no longer matter.

For starters, when a union activist sues a farmer or group of farmers, a settlement term they increasingly insist on is that the farmer waive the NLRA's exemption. Put differently, even though the NLRA doesn't force farmers to negotiate with unions, more and more farmers are being forced to treat their employees as if the exemption doesn't exist. That is, unless they want to pay hefty legal fees and be subject to burdensome discovery. Who needs a federal law when an expensive lawsuit can, via settlement, produce the same result? Second, many states are exploring or have already

206. "Beef Checkoff Case (R-CALF USA v. Perdue)," Case, Public Justice, last modified August 3, 2021, *https://food.publicjustice.net/case/beef-checkoff-case-r-calf-usa-v-perdue/*.

enacted laws that make unionizing under state law easier. While worker protections are and should be serious business, much of the rhetoric around farmworker organizing is premised on the narrative that the overwhelming majority of on-farm employees are exploited and have little to no job security. That narrative, combined with a lawsuit, makes for a costly cocktail.

The most recent legal development in the agriculture world is the ascendancy of anti-competitive conduct-based litigation, generally targeted at the largest multinational agricultural entities. Bayer, Corteva, Syngenta, and BASF have all been sued under these theories. In the protein sector, Cargill, JBS, National Beef, Smithfield Foods, Claxton Poultry, and Tyson have either received service of process or been the subject of investigations. Pilgrim's Pride, Sanderson Farms, and Koch Foods have too. In some of these cases, farmers serve as plaintiffs. State attorneys general have also weighed in to urge for more activity in this space.[207]

Consistent with the theme of this book, some of the loudest cheering for the antitrust litigation aimed squarely at some of American's largest food companies comes from entities that think farming needs to be revolutionized, or at least rethought, in the U.S. The National Sustainable Agriculture Coalition is one such organization.[208] In essay after essay, the NSAC suggests—or outright concludes—that the "status quo" of contemporary agriculture is not worth defending. "The modern U.S. food and agriculture system is designed *to maximize a narrow concept of economic efficiency* which fails to prioritize the well-being of small family farmers, rural

207. Wayne Stenehjem, email message to Attorney General Barr, May 5, 2020, available at: *https://www.iowaattorneygeneral.gov/media/cms/beef_antitrust_letter_20200505Barr__4D5075D98B205.pdf.*

208. National Sustainable Agriculture Coalition, "The Time is Ripe for Competition and Antitrust Reform in Agriculture," National Sustainable Agriculture Coalition, February 12, 2021, *https://sustainableagriculture.net/blog/the-time-is-ripe-for-competition-and-antitrust-reform-in-agriculture/.*

communities, or the land."[209] Given that perspective, why wouldn't NSAC urge for the use of market concentration legal theories to destroy it?

During its infancy, generally believed to be in the 1980s, agricultural law was mainly about how farmers and their creditors navigated the financial crisis of that period.[210] Over time, at least partly because of urbanization and closer coexistence of farms and non-farmers, and because of the increasing complexity of agribusiness, the issue list has grown. Production contracts and incentives. Risk management and crop insurance. Farm Bill and conservation program compliance. Liability for agritourism, hunting, and fishing. Farm labor law. Rules governing off-farm transportation. As if those issues weren't enough, farmers now face the reality of special interest groups using litigation to alter the agricultural landscape further.

No review of the rise of litigation affecting agriculture would be complete without at least mentioning the rise of the agricultural law curriculum in American law schools. In full disclosure, I have contributed to this phenomenon. Many years ago, I approached the dean of the University of North Carolina School of Law with what must have been a convincing case that the curriculum there should include an agricultural law course. That it would be taught by the general counsel of the State Department of Agriculture (me, at the time) was a bonus. And for me, the bonus was in the opportunity to interact with some of the sharpest budding legal minds in the country. My goal each year is to learn more from them than they do from me—and I have never been disappointed. One student taught

209. National Sustainable Agriculture Coalition, "Farmers Trapped in Unsustainable Cycle by Biotechnology, Seed Consolidation," National Sustainable Agriculture Coalition, July 9, 2021, *https://sustainableagriculture.net/blog/farmers-trapped-in-unsustainable-cycle-by-biotechnology-seed-consolidation/*.

210. The National Agricultural Law Center, *The Study of Agricultural Law in the United States: Education, Organization and Practice* (Arkansas: University of Arkansas School of Law, 1990), The National Agricultural Law Center, *https://nationalaglawcenter.org/wp-content/uploads/2013/06/hamilton_study.pdf*.

me the correct pronunciation of quinoa (keen´-wah). I am forever grateful. I actually like it.

The interest in ag law among legal students—many of whom have never even been on a farm—is just one more sign that those traditionally outside the food system are taking greater and greater interest in its direction. The interest among law professors is equally as instructive. Like some of the investors, politicians, international actors, and consumers examined elsewhere in this book, many of the professors dedicated to the study (and teaching) of ag law believe the current food and ag system in the United States is horribly broken.

From the "Food, Agriculture and the Environment: Law & Policy" course description at Duke University:

> *Most of us eat at least three times a day and, unless you are in extraordinary circumstances, those meals were produced within our national—and increasingly global—food and agriculture system. And it's a system that causes startling environmental harms; think water and air pollution, pesticides, greenhouse gases, non-human[e] animal welfare, deforestation, soil depletion, wetlands destruction, fisheries collapse, and on and on. Yet notions of "agricultural exceptionalism" exempt agriculture from many of our nation's environmental laws.*[211]

In other words, join us for a fourteen-week look at how agriculture is ruining the planet, and how it is completely avoiding regulatory scrutiny of any kind. It's farcical.

---

211. "636 Food, Agriculture and the Environment: Law & Policy," Study, Duke Law, last modified September 17, 2021, *https://law.duke.edu/academics/course/636*.

Like Duke, Vermont Law School is one of several law schools across the country that reflect the growing focus on agriculture and food law in the modern law school curricula. They offer a master's degree in agricultural law, which they refer to as a Master of Food and Agriculture Law and Policy. In their words, the MFALP degree program "is designed to educate future leaders in food and agricultural law and policy."[212]

Vermont Law's Center for Agriculture and Food Systems houses several initiatives aimed at "training the next generation of law and policy leaders to build a more sustainable and just food system."[213] One of those initiatives features a partnership with the Harvard Law School Food Law and Policy Clinic. The goal of the partnership is to examine "the potential for developing a cohesive national food strategy in the United States."[214]

Why, you may ask, do we need a national food strategy, and why would a law school in Vermont be the place to launch it? I'm glad you asked. The following explains why the school is so interested:

> *Regulation of the American food system is riddled with inequalities and inefficiencies. There is no federal "food" agency; instead, food is regulated by a range of agencies whose missions often conflict and overlap. Multiple agencies regulate food safety, production practices, agricultural workers, dietary guidelines, water pollution, and more.* **It's a patchwork approach**

212. "Master of Food and Agriculture Law and Policy (MFALP)," Masters Degrees, Vermont Law School, last modified September 22, 2021, *https://www.vermontlaw.edu/academics/degrees/masters/master-of-food-and-agriculture-law-and-policy-%28mfalp%29.*

213. "What We Offer," The Center for Agriculture and Food Systems, Vermont Law School, last modified September 22, 2021, *https://www.vermontlaw.edu/academics/centers-and-programs/center-for-agriculture-and-food-systems.*

214. "Blueprint for a National Food Strategy," CAFS Projects, Vermont Law School, last modified March 15, 2017, *https://www.vermontlaw.edu/academics/centers-and-programs/center-for-agriculture-and-food-systems/projects/blueprint-national-food.*

> **with dire consequences: simultaneous obesity and hunger; food insecurity and waste; a reliance on foreign labor and barriers to immigration; agriculture speeding climate change, which in turn threatens agriculture.** *[emphasis added] And the list goes on.*[215]

In short, the school training the next generation of farming and food law leaders believes the current system has produced atrocious results. Once again, just to be clear, if you're involved in production agriculture and are still reading, they are talking about you.

The Pace-NRDC Food Law Initiative sits at the Elisabeth Haub School of Law at Pace University in White Plains, New York. According to U.S. News and World Report, Pace is also home to the top environmental law program in the country. Their interest in agriculture? "The Pace-NRDC Food Law Initiative (FLI) supports the transition to a just and sustainable food system."[216] As a part of that work, they campaign for "transformative policy change" aimed at addressing the "inequities of the food system."

There are other examples. With equally as lofty ambitions and equally outraged masters. What is obvious here is that many legal scholars and law students are not attracted to the study of the agriculture and food system because they revere it. They want to rewire it.

Not every law school with an agriculture focus has a website with such dire warnings and commitment to saintly work. Iowa State, Drake, the University of Arkansas, and Michigan State, among others, offer multiple courses to prepare soon-to-be-licensed attorneys to counsel farmers and food system leaders in a more traditional sense. That said, for every program focused on helping a budding lawyer

215. "Blueprint for a National Food Strategy," CAFS Projects, Vermont Law School, last modified March 15, 2017, *https://www.vermontlaw.edu/academics/centers-and-programs/center-for-agriculture-and-food-systems/projects/blueprint-national-food*, (emphasis added).

216. "Pace-NRDC Food Law Initiative," Centers & Institutes, Pace University, last modified November 29, 2021, *https://law.pace.edu/pace-nrdc-food-law-initiative*.

understand present use value property tax discounts, there's at least one more focused on using the law—and therefore litigation—to battle inequities they view as blatantly apparent in today's agricultural complex.

Everywhere farmers turn, legal developments hold the potential to alter how they run their operations. Clean Water Act litigation. Endangered Species Act cases. Environmental Justice and Title VII of the Civil Rights Act. Labor law. All of the examples spelled out elsewhere in this chapter. The irony is that it is the legal framework and the rule of law that have given American agriculture such an advantage in pursuing its business. Enforceable contracts. Private property rights. Predictable liability environments. It appears that framework is being turned on its head. Those protections and foundations are now under attack.

Going forward, food and ag will be leveraged as a tool for social change, and much of that prying will occur in legal pleadings with farmers and food companies that are in the defendant slot of the case name. Ag system outsiders with a legal bent have learned that they can leverage legal action the same way they leverage the media, politics, and the legislative process. They issue reports. Write op-eds. Speak at conferences. Find a compelling plaintiff and tell their story over and over and over. They sponsor scholarships, internships, and clinics. And increasingly, they are winning. Even when they don't succeed in court, they consider the publicity they earn to be worth the trouble. The legal work is just part of the overall plan to dismantle modern American agriculture:

> *The legal work is a tool in the toolbox of a broader vision of what we want to see happen. There are certain times when strategic litigation can advance a campaign or long-term goal. It helps us push the broader organizing forward. It's a matter of matching*

> *the legal strategy with the organizing and legislative and communications strategy and making sure they're all aligned.*[217]

That's Public Justice again. They understand America's love affair with the law, and the earned media that goes along with filing a lawsuit. They also understand where the fault lines are in America's relationship with the agriculture sector, and they are working feverishly to exploit them.

217. Public Justice, "Fighting Factory Farm Gas from the Frontlines," *Public Justice*, April 6, 2021, *https://medium.com/food-project/fighting-factory-farm-gas-from-the-frontlines-aab1ccabd83*.

CHAPTER NINE

FARMERS WITHOUT BORDERS

It was April 26, 2017. A little before five o'clock in the afternoon. White House time.

I was the Special Assistant to the President for agriculture, and I had just helped the Secretary of Agriculture, who by that afternoon had been the Secretary for all of one day, navigate his way from the top floor of the Eisenhower Executive Office Building down into the West Wing of the White House to speak directly with President Trump. Uninvited.

Typically the Oval Office requires a reservation or, at least, call ahead seating. We did neither. Nobody had given us permission to be there. In fact, as we milled around outside the Oval waiting to, in my words to the receptionist "just get a word with the President about NAFTA," I only half-expected this desperate, long-shot plan to work.

Earlier that day, National Economic Council Director Gary Cohn had informed the NEC team at one of our early morning meetings that the President was set on unilaterally terminating NAFTA before the end of the week.[218] Nobody took the news harder than me. Gary shared my frustrations. But this one seemed to be locked down. I returned to my desk from our ritualistic huddle in Gary's office atop the second floor of the West Wing and stared at my business card. "Special Assistant to the President for Agriculture, Agriculture Trade, and Food Assistance." My job was to represent and, in my opinion, fight for the American farmer. And that farmer had grown increasingly dependent on international trade, particularly with Canada and Mexico. Just the rumor that NAFTA would be terminated had already unsettled markets, shook the commodity trade, and made my stomach feel like it does when I see blue lights in my rear-view mirror. Even if they are coming for someone else.

I phoned the chief of staff at USDA, Heidi Green, to share the news. Ever a step ahead, she had already heard the rumor regarding termination, which I confirmed. Fortunately for American agriculture, she had also already begun thinking about how to leverage Secretary Perdue and his by then two-days-old oath of office. We had all sat in the Roosevelt Room less than twenty-four hours earlier for the first Presidential Farmer Roundtable since Reagan had met with farmers after lifting the Russian wheat embargo in 1981. I was already exhausted from the hundreds of hours of work I had poured into that event. All the goodwill earned by getting a diverse group of farmers in to see President Trump within the first one hundred days of his administration was, I feared, about to go up in smoke.

218. NAFTA is the North American Free Trade Agreement, which for over twenty years had governed the trading relationship between the United States and two of its top three agricultural trading partners.

I do not remember precisely when the plan came into focus for Heidi and me, but it was brilliant. We would sneak the Secretary into the Oval and help him talk the President out of withdrawing from NAFTA.

That was it. That was the brilliant plan.

Cut us some slack. We had never had to secretly talk a United States President into reversing one of his major policy initiatives before. There was no playbook. No "go by." And forget Googling it.

My contribution to this effort was to get Secretary Perdue to the Oval, and to pray a lot that this was not a complete and total disaster. I was fairly certain that I would be fired if this effort capsized, or even if it went well. I made this point to Gary when I called him shortly before we stored our phones in the soundproof box just outside the Oval Office suite and tucked in to make our way to the President. Gary had already completed a pretty busy day himself, having briefed in the press room on the President's signature tax plan. To my best recollection, he was headed back to New York but was also working the phones to try to avert the unannounced NAFTA withdrawal. His words were to "go," and he promised that he would help me find work if needed.

So. There we were. A two-term Georgia governor turned ag Secretary and a farmer's kid from Autryville. Oh, and don't forget Tagalong Tim. That's Tim Murtaugh, who some two years later would depart as USDA's communications director to join the Trump re-elect operation and ultimately rise to be the 2020 campaign communications director. I distinctly remember having to tell Tim to keep up at least twice, as his credentials were meaningless within the White House unless he was attached to the Secretary or hosted by me.

We waited patiently to just poke our heads into the Oval. All we were hoping for was a few minutes. Like we were dropping by to say hello after church on a Sunday.

Fortunately for us, Secretary Perdue had hit it off with Trump personal bodyguard Keith Schiller during Cabinet tryouts in New York the previous November. Mr. Schiller had no objections to our unscheduled pop-in and proudly ensured we would be able to see the boss.

Unfortunately for us, Chief of Staff Reince Priebus appeared out of nowhere and was less charitable. Mr. Priebus marched us into the adjacent Cabinet room and rebuked us for thinking we could just walk up unannounced and get face time with the President. (I have no earthly idea where we would have gotten that idea.) During his lecture, I spent most of my time avoiding eye contact and looking for the light switch, which I never found. Tim, being much smarter than me, had disappeared again. He certainly was not there for Mr. Priebus's censure of the Secretary and me in the shadows of the Cabinet room. The Secretary navigated this dressing down beautifully, and we emerged still on track to slip in to see the President.

There are more details, but we eventually made it to the Resolute Desk. Informed by a tip from USDA Senior Adviser and former campaign aide Dr. Sam Clovis that the President liked maps, Secretary Perdue produced a color-coded United States map of the counties President Trump had carried in the election. The Midwest, which at least in an agricultural sense was the area most likely to be impacted by a NAFTA withdrawal, was a sea of red.

I will never forget Secretary Perdue affably explaining to the President that most farmers liked NAFTA and that they would be hurt without a more orderly transition to a different trade agreement. I chimed in from time to time with what I believed were very helpful and detailed factual statistics about where Canada and Mexico ranked as trading partners for some of our major commodities. I also remember frequently saying things like "that's right," and "that's for sure."

I will also never forget President Trump swiveling toward Tim to get his opinion. At that moment, Tim was a complete and total stranger to the President, and he had stationed himself along the perimeter of the Oval to avoid precisely the kind of interaction the President now sought.

"Is that true? Do the farmers like NAFTA?" asked the President.

"Yes. Yes, the farmers like NAFTA, Mr. President," replied Tim.

Over about a twenty-five minute period, we discussed a lot. And the President listened. In the meantime, more and more people gathered in the Oval to weigh in, at least partly because I had walked back and forth to ask Madeleine Westerhout to call for reinforcements to come help us make the case. Madeleine sat just outside the Oval, and upon approaching her the second time, she let me know we needed to wind things down. From time to time, the President would holler at her to find Peter Navarro and get him to the Oval. Madeleine had apparently already tried to reach him multiple times. At one point, Madeleine yelled back that she had called him on his cell and didn't get him. It was difficult to separate the banter between the two of them from that I was accustomed to in the tobacco fields of my youth.

It didn't matter. Secretary Perdue (and I) had already worked magic.

By the time this impromptu meeting ended, there must have been fifteen people standing around.[219] Most of them said very little, perhaps stunned that two sons of the South had pulled off what nobody before us had been able to do. The real credit here goes to President Trump, who absolutely loved his farmers.[220] On our way

219. I was always amazed at how intimate the Oval always felt, despite its physical size. It is, in reality, a large room.

220. Before, during, and after my tenure as his colleague, Secretary Perdue and I talked at length about how it was that President Trump was so proud of the support he received from the farming community. The Secretary chalked it up to the typical farmer's entrepreneurial spirit, something he said President Trump likely recognized and appreciated.

out, the President thanked the Secretary for coming in, making a point to say that he appreciated the perspective he had just been provided.

Over the next few hours, the notion that NAFTA would be renegotiated, not terminated, became the standard talking point. Secretary Perdue and I stuck around for a trade meeting in the Roosevelt Room, where we discussed the current state of play—which we had just altered. About halfway through that meeting, we were interrupted by Jared Kushner, who came to reinforce the conclusion that NAFTA would be renegotiated, not terminated. He ended with something akin to "I just want to make sure everyone in this room understands that," followed by a long pause. If there were any folks who harbored uncertainties about the finality of the decision, Jared had cleared the air as only he could do.

Not a bad day's work.

The President would later growl that he wished he had been allowed to withdraw, but in the end, he got a new trade deal with Canada and Mexico that received wide, bipartisan support. It was arguably one of his capstone legislative achievements. And the Secretary and I got to keep our jobs.

Let's be clear. President Trump, in listening to Secretary Perdue, saved NAFTA. I was a mere wingman.

To this day, it surprises me that anyone would think they need to tell the Special Assistant to the President for Agriculture and Agriculture Trade that trade is important to the ag economy. After all, I believe I am quite likely the only guy from Sampson County who ever risked his career to save a trade deal. Over the next couple of years, I would hear aggies from all across the U.S. take precious time to tell Secretary Perdue just how critical ag trade was to their subsector. He was always gracious and agreed. But the fact that American agriculture has become increasingly dependent on having markets outside the U.S. is, in agricultural knowledge, akin to the star in the middle of the bingo board. It's a freebie. A given. Everyone already knows that. I did not need to hear it, nor did the Secretary.

This story does more than demonstrate my appreciation for international markets. It also reveals just how vulnerable American farmers have become when it comes to key decisions regarding those international markets. In this case, a sitting American president was days away from upending the most American ag-friendly trade agreement in the world, and most of the ag community was not even aware the fuse on the ticking time bomb had been lit. Note how this fits in with the theme of this book. Notwithstanding the implications for agriculture, the agreement that established the rules of engagement for two of our biggest three export markets was about to be tossed. Had it been two weeks earlier, the country might have seen a different result.

Depending on the year, generally three out of every four rows of American-grown cotton are shipped outside the United States. Every other row of soybeans goes the same way, not to mention the soybeans that are processed into beef, chicken, and pork products before they are exported.[221] Including ethanol and distillers dried grains, at least one in five rows of corn. Half of all wheat, sorghum, and rice.[222] Twenty-eight percent of our total pork volume, one in ten beef cattle, and one of every eight chickens is bound for a mouth outside the United States.[223]

221. To be clear, I'm not talking here about some exotic form of meatloaf. It's a joke. I'm referring to the grains fed to farm animals so that those animals will grow to a point that they are suitable for slaughter. And export. And being eaten.

222. Keith Good, "U.S. Ag Exports to China: Soybeans and Corn," *Farm Policy News—Illinois,* June 8, 2017, *https://farmpolicynews.illinois.edu/2017/06/u-s-ag-exports-china-soybeans-corn/*.

223. "Percentage of U.S. Agricultural Products Exported," Data and Analysis, U.S. Department of Agriculture, last modified May 30, 2018, *https://www.fas.usda.gov/data/percentage-us-agricultural-products-exported*; and Christine McCracken, "Ag Allies: Latest Developments in Trade," (webinar, NC Chamber, November 30, 2011).

Those statistics are impressive. But the purpose of this chapter is not to catalog U.S. ag exports. That, you *can* Google. The point here is to observe what I call the boomerang effect of American agriculture's increasing dependence on foreign markets. When we become dependent on selling product into the global marketplace, we necessarily become more dependent on the global marketplace's customs, standards, and whims. In other words, when we invite ourselves to the world market, even if we are bringing dinner, we simultaneously invite the foreign customer's preferences, peculiarities, and politics back into our farms.

So just what are those outside forces that we've now invited into American agriculture? Besides the ones on either side of Seventeenth Street in Washington, D.C.?[224]

There is no more qualified person to answer that question than Sharon Bomer Lauritson. Sharon is now the founder of AgTrade Strategies LLC and a past leader of the Biotechnology Innovation Organization's Food and Agriculture Section. I got to know her because of a role she filled in between those two posts, while she was the assistant United States trade representative for Agricultural Affairs and Commodity Policy at the U.S. Trade Representative's Office. She served in that capacity while I was working at the White House. At other points in her career, she worked at USDA, on the Hill, and for United Fresh. (And you thought *I* had trouble keeping a job.)

Sharon's thirty years of experience and accomplishments could fill an entire book of their own. U.S.-China Phase One. U.S.-Japan. U.S.-Australia. U.S.-EU. U.S.-Mexico-Canada. U.S.-Colombia. TPP. TPP withdrawal. U.S.-Korea. WTO ministerials and disputes galore. You get the point. If there's an influence on domestic agriculture

224. The United States Trade Representative's Office sits just across Seventeenth Street from the Eisenhower Executive Office Building, a mere 350 feet from the lower entrance to the West Wing.

from an international market, or an American attempt to work through it, Sharon has seen it.

Let's start with what Sharon shared with me that shocked me. I was prepared to write about protectionism, the term often used to describe a country's preference for its domestic producers over those attempting to export into that country. I had planned to give you several examples, carefully peeling the onion of how the craftiest of our trading partners couch pure market protectionism in creative nomenclature. Sharon practically yawned. "All countries protect farmers. They are different only in how they do it." In other words, put protectionism on the list with phytosanitary conditions and grading standards. It matters. And every country speaks their own version. But it is just part of the global sales field. Always has been, and likely always will be. In almost any corner of the world, constituents prefer their own farmers over those from elsewhere.

Ambassador Gregg Doud, who served as the chief agricultural negotiator in the U.S. Trade Representative's Office during the Trump Administration, and who therefore worked closely with Sharon, generally agrees. What Gregg and Sharon further agree on is that there are forces operating within many of the United States' target markets that present an even larger long-term threat to the interests of the American farmer. And possibly as equally large threat to global food security itself.

Look no further than the European Union for a movement that appears to be squarely aimed at convincing the world that America's version of agricultural ingenuity is misguided. Importantly, the EU is number four in U.S. agricultural export markets, with over $12 billion in product sold there in 2020 alone.[225]

The EU's Common Agriculture Policy (CAP) is about the closest thing the Europeans have to a Farm Bill. In their words,

225. "European Union," Europe and Eurasia, U.S. Department of Agriculture, last modified November 29, 2021, *https://www.fas.usda.gov/regions/european-union*.

it is a "partnership between agriculture and society, and between Europe and its farmers."[226] A 2021 rewrite of the CAP has now been ratified, but it has been criticized by European environmentalists for not incorporating more of the ambitions within the European Green Deal. Work on the Green Deal policy proposal continues, in line with the EU's goal to become climate-neutral by 2050.

The Farm to Fork (F2F) strategy is a part of the European Green Deal. In fact, if parts of the Green Deal are implemented, they would inevitably override part of the policy settled in the latest version of the CAP. The aspirations of the F2F strategy are impressive, even if presently unrealistic: (1) reduce pesticide use by 50 percent, (2) reduce soil nutrient loss by 50 percent and therefore reduce fertilizer use by 20 percent, (3) reduce antibiotic use for farm animals by 50 percent, and (4) transition 25 percent of the EU's agricultural land to organic farming.[227] All of this is designed to produce an agriculture system that is "fair, healthy, and environmentally friendly."[228]

EU Green Deal Chief Frans Timmermans says the quiet part out loud. In referring to the Green Deal as an "ecoscheme," he mentions that the goal is to "get away from counting success just by the number of wagons of food we produce."[229]

Of course, Mr. Timmermans's admonition is not entirely unwarranted. Sustainability and environmental preservation should be hallmarks of a balanced farm and food system. The problem here is that EU policy makers appear to be poised to extort European

226. "The common agricultural policy at a glance," CAP at a glance, European Commission, last modified October 6, 2021, *https://ec.europa.eu/info/food-farming-fisheries/key-policies/common-agricultural-policy/cap-glance_en*.

227. European Commission, *Farm to Fork Strategy* (Europe: European Commission, 2020), European Commission Action Plan, available at *https://ec.europa.eu/food/system/files/2020-05/f2f_action-plan_2020_strategy-info_en.pdf*.

228. It will also help the Europeans tackle obesity, as it will undoubtedly create food scarcity in a way generally not experienced there in over fifty years.

229. EURural, "Getting the CAP Strategic Plans done: the voice of regions and stakeholders," YouTube video, 9:58, posted May 10, 2021, *https://www.youtube.com/watch?v=7kjmwdhrCs0*.

farmers into reducing production without any real plan to address the food scarcity that would come with it. As one divinity school professor put it, "Before you can admonish someone that man cannot live by bread alone, you have to make sure that they have bread."

Even Europe's own farmers are concerned about the possible carnage. Copa & Cogeca, the EU's version of American Farm Bureau and the National Council of Farmer Cooperatives combined, has attempted to challenge the strategy without criticizing the ultimate goal: "Targets alone are not a strategy unless they are accompanied by EU measures on how to achieve them on the ground, in a practical and realistic manner."[230]

American officials are generally uniform in their criticism of the F2F approach. In 2020, Trump's Secretary of Agriculture penned an op-ed that pointedly suggested Europe had "forgotten the 'farm' in 'farm to fork.'" He also wrote that the EU's stand was "one based more on 'political science' than demonstrated agricultural science."[231] In 2021, Biden's Secretary of agriculture expressed the same resolve. "There is a concern in many parts of the world that sustainable agriculture could result in a reduction" in food production, Vilsack said. "We believe that actually, a more sustainable agriculture can also be a more productive agriculture and can, in fact, meet the needs and demands of a growing global population."[232] Vilsack has wisely spearheaded a productivity coalition that—in the international sphere—pushes back on the EU's F2F strategies.

Why all the concern over the EU's ag policy? After all, if they want to shrink their agriculture industry, isn't that good for American farmers who enjoy exporting there?

---

230. "Press Releases," News, Copa-Cogeca, last modified November 29, 2021, *https://copa-cogeca.eu/press-releases.*

231. Sonny Perdue, "Europe Has Forgotten the 'Farm' in 'Farm to Fork'," *EuObserver,* October 5, 2020, *https://euobserver.com/opinion/149489.*

232. Steve Davies, "Vilsack touts new ag productivity coalition as counter to EU," *AgriPulse,* September 16, 2021, *https://www.agri-pulse.com/articles/16487-vilsack-touts-new-ag-productivity-coalition-as-counter-to-eu.*

Not so fast. If F2F is implemented as quickly and aggressively as the European farmers themselves fear, two immediate problems arise for farmers in the lower forty-eight. Many EU member countries would immediately legislate that imports must meet the same standards as crops grown domestically. In fact, French President Emmanuel Macron recently stated as much: "We cannot ask our farmers to make more efforts and, the next day, import products coming from regions that" don't undertake those same efforts.[233] This statement was made during, and I am not making this up, the "Great Rendez-vous of Food Sovereignty."[234]

The second problem is that the EU would continue its successful track record of exporting its policy preferences around the world to keep its own exports competitive. A September 29, 2021, Politico article referred to the coming "Cold War" between the U.S. and EU as both collectives push their preferred narratives for farm and food sustainability. "These days, trade is all about the battle for international standards, and the U.S. has long smarted over how the EU has flexed its muscle through trade policy to impose global food norms, including the geographical indication labels that protect its premium brands like Champagne and Parma ham."[235]

Kip Tom, who from a production agriculture standpoint is one of the most qualified U.S. ambassadors we have ever deployed to the United Nations Agencies for Food and Agriculture, has been open about the fact that the Europeans are not "with us" on the mission field here. In fact, they are against us, and want to challenge the way we produce crops, livestock, and protect the environment.

---

233. Gabriela Galindo, "Macron's Recipe for Fair-Trade Food," Politico, May 27, 2021, *https://www.politico.eu/article/emmanuel-macron-fair-trade-food-gastronomy-france-election-2022/*.

234. At least in France there is never an expectation that the farmers would be taken more seriously than the foodies.

235. Eddy Wax and Emma Anderson, "The Transatlantic Relationship Descends into a Food Fight," Politico, September 29, 2021, *https://www.politico.eu/article/farm-to-fork-europe-united-states-food-agriculture-trade-climate-change/*.

Kip pointed out the irony: "We've been working 'within our planetary boundaries' and they're (the EU) probably twenty years behind us. Nonetheless, they act like they are leading on this and the rest of the world is watching them."[236]

To put it more plainly, once Brussels sufficiently hampers the EU's food production capability, they will turn quickly to export their policy. History shows they are likely to succeed in that quest. The question for the American farmer and food processor becomes whether they can do anything to stop it.

Gregg Doud, the former ag ambassador in the U.S. Trade Representative's Office and current vice president of global situational awareness at Aimpoint, put it this way:

> *The European agriculture sector is in decline. It can be debated as to whether this is an inevitable progression or mainly due to the European Union's insistence on a regulatory regime that significantly constrains innovation and the use of modern technologies. Despite this decline, the EU, in collaboration with the NGO community, continues to have an outsized influence on how other countries regulate their own agricultural industries. It is time for this to end before damage is done to the world's ability to continue to produce an abundance of food. If the EU insists on inflicting its Farm to Fork Initiative on itself, that's its prerogative. However, inflicting this regressive agenda on others, including developing nations, is despicable.*

---

236. Chris Clayton, "Kip Tom: UN Direction Flawed," *Ohio's Country Journal*, July 27, 2021, *https://ocj.com/2021/07/kip-tom-un-direction-flawed/*.

In sum, while the phrase "food sovereignty" is bantered about by our friends across the Atlantic, they appear intent on pushing other countries to adopt policies that make them something closer to "food subservient." Note the triple play. Domestic production becomes hamstrung, European imports are favored, and American imports are all but off the table. So far, the Africans have resisted the senseless urge to follow suit. Parts of South America—yes, South America—seem less prepared to resist.

Another example of a country constraining innovation is Mexico. Despite language in the USMCA trade agreement meant to hasten the biotechnology approval process, Mexican President Andrés Manuel López Obrador announced in December of 2020 that he plans to ban both glyphosate and transgenic corn for human consumption in Mexico by 2024. The results could be disastrous for Mexican farmers for whom access to existing and emerging genetic engineering technology will now be withheld, and for food prices, given that conventional or organic corn will likely cost more per bushel to obtain in the Mexican market than its trait-altered counterpart. As is the case in Europe, some farmers in Mexico oppose the idea of a glyphosate or GMO ban, as they fear it will lock them out of the market for developing corn technology that holds promises of greater efficiency and profitability for their farms.

Let's count the reasons this is a step backward. First, it violates the recently negotiated USMCA trade pact. Second, it will likely, in the end, hurt Mexican farmers more than it does any farmers elsewhere. Third, it will raise the price of corn in Mexico, which will undoubtedly have an impact on food security. And finally, note the double standard. GMO corn for livestock feed would still be permitted, at least as of the time of writing this book. None of those arguments are likely to stop implementation of President López Obrador's plans, however.

The President's decree certainly has the potential to eventually impact the United States' ability to export into the Mexican corn market, which is where we send between 25 to 40 percent of our corn exports every year. The bigger problem, though, is the policy's potential threat to food security. American farmers could certainly pivot to continue serving the Mexican market, even if the ban were extended to corn used for livestock consumption. Would this result in a resurgence of weed-management techniques that are less carbon friendly than those currently used on U.S. farms? Probably. And would it result in a reduction of yields? Undoubtedly, yes.

It is not just countries or pacts of countries. The alphabet soup of international organizations sometimes take counterintuitive views of agricultural innovation and abundance. One such organization—which seems to look at American's agricultural abundance with enmity, as opposed to admiration—is the World Health Organization. Clearly a loud voice in the international conversation, the WHO could easily be an advocate for the cutting-edge technology deployed in high-tech American agriculture. But it generally isn't. Rather than seeing agriculture as an ally to combatting hunger, it is increasingly promoting the view that agriculture is a public health menace. Take it from them:

> *Some agricultural policies can also contribute to unhealthy diets and unsafe food, including policies that do not address the use of antibiotics in animal husbandry and the use of harmful chemicals in pesticides, as well as specialization in outputs that are readily transformed into processed foods high in saturated fats, trans fat, salt and/or free sugars.*[237]

237. World Health Organization, *Health 2020: Agriculture and health through food safety and nutrition* (Europe: World Health Organization, 2015), World Health Organization Sector Brief on Agriculture. *https://www.euro.who.int/__data/assets/pdf_file/0016/324610/Health-2020-Agriculture-and-health-through-food-safety-and-nutrition-en.pdf*, page 5.

Here's a shorter version: "Our food systems are making us sick."[238] Just to be clear, they are talking about U.S. agriculture here. They flatly ignore that U.S. policy has addressed antibiotics in animal production, regulates crop chemistry as closely as any country in the world, and produces what the market demands.

While the WHO's ostensible focus on combatting non-communicable disease itself is difficult to criticize, it appears to be coming at the expense of the fight against hunger. That challenge still plagues millions in the United States and around the world, and to presume that it can be solved by eliminating the modern food system and its advancements is flatly nonsensical.

We can all hope for progress in reducing things in the non-communicable disease category like obesity, cancer, and heart disease, and we should all be willing to listen to evidence of how we can contribute to that progress. But surely such gains should be attainable without resorting to an annihilation of the current food system, particularly the American one that has produced so much.

WHO officials likely disagree: "Today, our food systems are making us ill, driving climatic change and undermining the health of ecosystems and the essential services on which our health and well-being depend."[239] Unfortunately, the WHO is one of many influential organizations operating under the assumption that our food systems are broken and getting worse, and they have been at the forefront of calls to radically rethink farming and food. Once again, the WHO:

---

238. World Health Organization, "New coalitions announced at the UN Food Systems Summit to increase access to healthy diets from sustainable food systems," *World Health Organization,* September 23, 2021, *https://www.who.int/news/item/23-09-2021-new-coalitions-announced-at-the-un-food-systems-summit-to-increase-access-to-healthy-diets-from-sustainable-food-systems.*

239. "Food systems delivering better health: executive summary," Overview, World Health Organization, last modified July 29, 2021, *https://www.who.int/publications/i/item/9789240031814.*

> *The evidence is clear, urgent and compelling: 2021 and beyond offer a unique opportunity to redesign food systems for better health in a number of major international forums and conferences on biodiversity, food systems, nutrition and climate change. There is momentum and a willingness on the part of many actors to engage and work towards this shift in food, health and natural systems.*[240]

The 2021 United Nations' Food Systems Summit was one of the opportunities WHO had in mind. The summit, described by UN Secretary General António Guterres as an opportunity for "radical reform" and sometimes casually referred to as the "Paris Climate Agreement for Food," took an alarmingly bombastic approach. Its organizers referred to "game changers" that they believed were necessary to feed the world while staying within "planetary boundaries."[241] That "planetary boundaries" nonsense arose from a 2019 study published in the *Lancet* that popularized the term. That study was funded by a billionaire plant-based-diet activist, who just so happened to be appointed to lead a key pillar of the summit's preparation.

You won't be shocked to learn, then, that one of the game-changing solutions put forth for consideration at the summit, Solution 15, was authored by a group that wants to cut the consumption of animal products by 50 percent by 2040. This bias is readily apparent when you read the litany of their complaints against animal agriculture.[242]

240. *Ibid.*

241. Agricultural Retailers Association, American Feed Industry Association and American Frozen Food Institute, email message to Secretary of State Blinken and Secretary of Agriculture Vilsack, April 22, 2021, available at: *https://static1.squarespace.com/static/5faeee45a363746603d1c6e1/t/60f081befaec3a5c4dac73fa/1626374591048/Meeting+Request+re+UN+Food+Systems+Summit+April+22+2021.pdf.*

242. United Nations—Food Systems Summit 2021, *Action Track 2: Shift to sustainable and healthy consumption patterns* (United Nations, 2021), United Nations Synthesis Report of Game Changing Solutions, available at: *https://www.un.org/sites/un2.un.org/files/unfss_at2_synthesis_propositions_round1.pdf.*

No wonder one commentator referred to the summit as a "many tenacled beast." While the summit ultimately did not endorse specific solutions, a cursory review of its inputs shows a disproportionate emphasis on, and shaky evidence to support, eliminating staples like meat, milk, and eggs. Breakfast would never be the same.

Before the summit, National Milk Producers Federation President and CEO Jim Mulhern put it this way:

> *Animal agriculture plays an important role in providing a sustainable source of nutrition that's critical for healthy diets and communities as well as a healthy planet, and we are encouraged by the many statements by world leaders today recognizing this important fact. . . .*
>
> *Some have viewed the summit as an opportunity to issue lengthy lists of do's and don'ts to the farmers worldwide who work hard every day to feed us all. . . . Rather than trying to impose a uniform, misguided ideology on how the world eats, farms and produces food, we all need to do our part to use limited resources wisely and efficiently to feed a growing world population in environmentally sound ways.*[243]

In other words, we are with you on the end goal, but the hard work is in selecting and then navigating the means we will use to get there. Kudos to Mr. Mulhern.

Former Missouri Farm Bureau President Blake Hurst, who is also a farmer and greenhouse grower in the northwest part of the state, poetically summarized how most American farmers feel

243. Jim Mulhern, NMPF and USDEC Joint Statement on UN Food Systems Summit, *Oklahoma Farm Report,* September 24, 2021, *http://oklahomafarmreport.com/wire/news/2021/09/03404_JointDairyStatement09242021_081644.php#.YalHQtBKg2x.*

about all the excitement surrounding the Food Systems Summit in an opinion piece for Agri-Pulse.

> *Come to find out, humanity has been suffering from a food system that is failing miserably by every measure that matters. We farmers have a lot to answer for, and the United Nations is just the organization to hold us to account. Hunger is increasing, and, according to the publicity surrounding the Summit, our present system of producing food is neither sustainable, inclusive, nor supportive of "smallholders." As a society we are not just obese, but wasteful.*

Mr. Hurst, as intelligent as he is determined, went on to point out just how drastic the gains in agriculture have been over the last few decades, before sarcastically succumbing to the narrative pushed throughout all the Summit hoopla:

> *But it's all been for naught, according to the experts lined up for the Summit, and we have to do better if we are to meet the 17 Sustainable Development Goals outlined by the United Nations. The Food System must change if we are to provide for a future with food produced by millions of smallholders . . . [who provide] healthy and nutritious food for local consumers, all without the use of herbicides, insecticides, or worst of all, genetically modified seed.*[244]

Without regard to whether you find the goals and narrative of a food systems summit to be worthy or convincing, what is undeniable

244. Blake Hurst, Opinion: A Farmer's Perspective on the Food Systems Summit, Agri-Pulse, June 25, 2021, *https://www.agri-pulse.com/articles/16094-opinion-a-farmers-perspective-on-the-food-systems-summit.*

is that convenings on the current and future state of the world food system, typically shrouded in gloom, are now a mainstay at the international level. As a result of the summit, more than 150 countries made commitments to "transform their food systems, while championing greater participation and equity, especially amongst farmers, women, youth and indigenous groups."[245] Going forward, the UN will work with its Rome-based Food and Agriculture Organization, the International Fund for Agricultural Development, and the World Food Programme to coordinate all the follow-up items on the task list.[246] The United States committed $10 billion to the effort, with half of that to be invested in the U.S. and the other half dedicated to fight global food insecurity through the already existing (and successful) Feed the Future initiative.[247]

One of the individuals I've learned to rely upon to help me cut through all the pomp and circumstance of the now common international conclaves dedicated to reforming the food system is Melissa San Miguel. Melissa is head of Americas for the global strategic communications and public affairs consultancy Red Flag. She previously served as the senior director for global strategies at the Grocery Manufacturers Association and began her career in the U.S. State Department, ultimately serving as Special Assistant to the Under Secretary for Economic Growth, Energy, and the Environment. Melissa has seen her fair share of these sorts of gatherings as a business representative and from the perspective of a diplomat

245. "World leaders commit to tackling global hunger, climate change and biodiversity loss at historic UN Food Systems Summit," Press Release, United Nations, last modified September 23, 2021, *https://www.un.org/en/food-systems-summit/news/world-leaders-commit-tackling-global-hunger-climate-change-and-biodiversity-loss*.

246. "Secretary-General's Chair Summary and Statement of Action on the UN Food Systems Summit," Statement, United Nations, last modified September 23, 2021, *https://www.un.org/en/food-systems-summit/news/making-food-systems-work-people-planet-and-prosperity*.

247. "Administrator Samantha Power and Secretary of Agriculture Tom Vilsack at the United Nations Food Systems Summit," News and Information, USAID, last modified September 23, 2021, *https://www.usaid.gov/news-information/speeches/sep-23-2021-samantha-power-and-secretary-agriculture-tom-vilsack-food-systems-summit*.

sitting behind the placard reading "United States" at some of these convenings.

Every farmer in America would like Melissa, and we are fortunate that she served us so well while in government. Discussing the international food policy network, Melissa points out the common threads that constitute an absurd yet nearly unquestioned consensus in today's global food policy debate:

1. Problems with the current food system far outnumber its positive attributes.
2. Producing plentiful food is now a problem—food systems provide too many calories but simultaneously not enough nutrition.[248]
3. Legitimate views and evidence related to food should be almost exclusively the domain of non-governmental organizations and academics (but only those who hold the "right" views). Governments should exclude anyone with a business interests from public discourse (never mind democratic rule-making norms), perhaps including their own economic, trade, and agriculture experts.
4. "Public health" is too important to be left to the "whim of consumer choice."[249] As one leading U.S. "public health"

248. Note the irony: The plenty that farmers are so proud of is now actively identified as the problem. The current food system is simultaneously overly generous with calories and insufficiently dense with nutrition.

249. From the EAT-Lancet report: "Faced with challenges, policy makers might initially implement soft policy interventions, such as consumer advice, information, education, or, in the case of food, labelling. These interventions assume that consumer actions will generate sufficient change and are slow in effect unless mass public interest in change exists. However, the scale of change to the food system is unlikely to be successful if left to the individual or the whim of consumer choice. This change requires reframing at the population and systemic level. By contrast, hard policy interventions include laws, fiscal measures, subsidies and penalties, trade reconfiguration, and other economic and structural measures." "Food in the Anthropocene: the EAT–Lancet Commission on healthy diets from sustainable food systems," The Lancet Commissions, *The Lancet*, last modified February 2, 2019, *https://www.thelancet.com/action/showPdf?pii=S0140-6736%2818%2931788-4* (pg. 478).

advocate has said, "We have to get rid of the unhealthy food before we get people to eat the healthy food."[250]

5. "Hard policy" tools are necessary to force better food choices on everyone.[251]

For a variety of reasons, agriculture and food stakeholders in the United States seem to be mostly playing catch-up in understanding this powerful (but wrong) consensus. Melissa says the frogs started boiling decades ago and that early complacency on issues like Chile's stop signs to label unhealthy food only gave the movement momentum.

The way statistics and human mortality work, something will always be the leading cause of death—fewer people in the modern world die young, smoking has fallen out of favor, but eating remains a fixture, and it turns out people are living longer, more prosperous lives. They are also eating more along the way (which, judging across the historical continuum, we would have surely considered a sign of progress). Not to mention that organizations like WHO failed spectacularly to contain infectious disease, which ironically upended many food supply chains around the world. As public health cast around for a new raison d'être, controlling diets proved irresistible.

As Melissa puts it, "Activists gotta activate, and regulators gotta regulate." Sooner or later, activism and regulation come home to roost.

Allow me to once again note that international pressure on domestic production practices can arise in a number of ways. It was

250. Laura Reiley, "Latin America's war on obesity could be a model for U.S.," *The Washington Post,* July 16, 2019, *https://www.washingtonpost.com/business/2019/07/16/latin-americas-war-obesity-could-be-model-us/.*

251. By some definitions, even food warning labels like stop signs and other marketing restrictions don't go far enough. "Public health" wants taxes to make foods deemed undesirable more expensive, subsidies for production of foods public health advocates approve of and penalties on those they don't, and trade agreements that preference certain foods and erect barriers to trading others.

the WHO's International Agency for Research on Cancer that, in March of 2015, concluded that Monsanto's popular herbicide Roundup was a "probable carcinogen."[252] Writing for *Forbes*, Geoffrey Kabat noted that this conclusion "goes against the assessment of every other agency that has evaluated the compound, including the U.S. Environmental Protection Agency, the European Food Safety Authority, and the World Health Organization, of which IARC is a part."[253] Mr. Kabat's article refers to the IARC's "glyphosate-gate scandal." As already discussed in Chapter 8, the IARC's conclusions weighed heavily in litigation that has already had profound implications for herbicide choice in the United States.[254]

To summarize, there are pivotal "future of food" conversations happening all around the world. And by no means have I captured all the players here. The World Economic Forum, the World Business Council for Sustainable Development, and others have all raised questions about how it is we plan to feed the planet without killing it first. Just because American farmers haven't heard of them doesn't mean they won't be affected by them. Some of them are rooted in protectionism. Others are based on concerns about the environment. Or malnutrition. Or something else. The bottom line is that our increasing reliance on global markets makes us increasingly vulnerable to the political and policy movements afoot in those markets.

---

252. World Health Organization—International Agency for Research on Cancer, *IARC Monographs Volume 112: evaluation of five organophosphate insecticides and herbicides* (World Health Organization, 2015), International Agency for Research on Cancer Monographs Volume 112, available at: *https://www.iarc.who.int/wp-content/uploads/2018/07/MonographVolume112-1.pdf.*

253. Geoffrey Kabat, "IARC's Glyphosate-gate Scandal," *Forbes,* October 23, 2017, *https://www.forbes.com/sites/geoffreykabat/2017/10/23/iarcs-glyphosate-gate-scandal/?sh=4d4ab1851abd.*

254. Stand by for more. IARC concluded in 2019 that night shift work posed similar cancer-inducing risks. Thomas Erren, et al., "IARC 2019: "'Night Shift Work' Is Probably Carcinogenic: What About Disturbed Chronobiology in All Walks of Life?," *Journal of Occupational Medicine and Toxicology,* November 27, 2019, *https://occup-med.biomedcentral.com/articles/10.1186/s12995-019-0249-6.*

Back to that meeting in the Oval. Not incidentally, we made the mistake of not collecting the color-coded maps after the meeting was over. They were photographed extensively (and apparently were the topic of lively conversation) when the President spoke with Reuters reporters later that same afternoon. As of the writing of this book, if you Google "April 26, 2017," "Reuters," and "maps," you can probably see them for yourself. The President would ask Madeleine to bring out "the map" many times over the ensuing years, but never were they more useful to American farmers than they were the day Secretary Perdue, Tim, and I forgot to make an appointment before dropping in to see the President.

On the international level, American agriculture needs to become more accustomed to showing up and changing the trajectory of discussions. With or without a reservation.

CHAPTER TEN

Extra! Extra! Read All about It!

Andy Curliss. There was a time when if that name showed up on caller ID, it would send chills down the spines of elected officials, their communications staffers, and even their lawyers. In 2016, that was all I really knew about him. I would come to learn much more.

Andy was a prize-winning and dogged investigative reporter for what was, at the time, my home state's most politically influential newspaper. His work is credited with directly influencing public policy outcomes but is even more famous among my peers for how it directly influenced personnel decisions. Mainly resignations.[255]

255. "NC House Speaker's Chief of Staff resigns," News, WCNC, last modified April 27, 2012, *https://www.wcnc.com/article/news/local/nc-house-speakers-chief-of-staff-resigns/275-373398672.*

At least one conviction.[256] By some counts, as many as five. Many of us whose backgrounds involved work for elected officials respected Andy. He was not a hack. But that didn't mean we had to like him.

When I was chief of staff for Senator Thom Tillis, who at the time was a member of the U.S. Senate Agriculture Committee, I remember exactly where I was standing in the Dirksen Senate Office Building when I received a call from a prominent home state pork producer who informed me that the North Carolina Pork Council had selected Andy to be its next CEO. I was flabbergasted. How in the world did this industry, which relies so heavily on engagement with regulators and elected officeholders, ever expect the very people Andy had targeted over the years to now engage productively with him? Good luck with that.

Over time, Andy proved his mettle and then some. Much of his work in the agriculture space has uncovered information about and brought attention to some of the very outside forces I write about in this book. A higher-level accomplishment—that I'm not even sure Andy or the ag community fully appreciates—is that he has helped many in agriculture understand that the pressures we are feeling are *not* a purely natural phenomenon. They are organized, planned, and calculated, and perhaps most shockingly, they are extraordinarily well funded. What we have learned in spades is that there are many parties seeking to influence the food system, and they are doing so strategically. They have learned to leverage our institutions—and sometimes the rot within those institutions—to their advantage.[257]

256. Andrew Curliss, "Former N.C. Gov. Easley Pleads Guilty to Campaign Charges," *McClatchy*, November 23, 2010, *https://www.mcclatchydc.com/news/politics-government/article24601582.html.*

257. For an absolutely splendid expose into the decay of many of our cherished institutions, I highly recommend Yuval Levin's book, "A Time to Build." Of particular relevance here, Levin eloquently describes the tendency of our modern-day culture to reward "those who can successfully claim the mantle of the outsider." As he explains, this is problematic since outsiders rarely even know how to reform an institution they have no experience in. In his view, and I agree with him, "unabashed insiders" are much more likely to be successful in reforming an institution than a wailing outsider. Levin, Yuval. *A Time to Build: From Family and Community to Congress and the Campus, How*

Saying they build coalitions is an understatement. They are movement architects.[258]

One such moment of clarity for me came about in the late summer of 2019, a day after the *News & Observer* in Raleigh, the very newspaper where Andy had done so much knuckle-cracking work earlier in his career, published a front-page, Sunday-edition story entitled "Complaints Disappear and Reappear, but the Awful Stench from NC Hog Farms Remains." The story was suspiciously well-timed to add fuel to the fire of simmering litigation over the presence of the swine industry and its impact in the communities where bacon—nature's most perfect plant-based food—is made.[259]

The premise put forth in the article was that North Carolina's hog farms were woefully under-policed. The "journalists" clearly wanted the reader to walk away with the impression that North Carolina regulators weren't doing their jobs and were failing to adequately monitor hog farms. Or more accurately, hog farmers. To get the reader to that point, the writers compared the complaints made about hog farmers in North Carolina to the complaints made about animal agriculture in completely different states, including complaints filed about completely different animals. This amounted to a classic apples and oranges misstep that treated hogs and cattle and chickens and big states and small states all as somehow equal. That's bad. But worse, the article didn't even acknowledge a most important fact: the state of North Carolina is the leader in *preventative* regulation, with inspectors visiting farms and conducting on-site reviews that number in the thousands every year. Sharing sparse complaint data—that is, inspections that occur solely as the result of a complaint—while ignoring a

---

Recommitting to Our Institutions Can Revive the American Dream. Basic Books, 2020. (pp. 25, 55).

258. We, on the other hand, seem to be mostly preoccupied with winning the Farm Credit hat giveaway at the end of the meeting. (But hey, they are nice hats!)

259. I also stole this joke from Andy. Barry Yeoman, "Complaints Disappear and Reappear, but the Awful Stench from NC Hog Farms Remains," *News & Observer*, Updated Aug. 30, 2019, https://www.newsobserver.com/news/business/article234482987.html.

vigorous and copious *regular* inspection process left the reader with an impression that did not match reality.[260]

But that was the point.

A complete takedown of the falsehoods in the story is not necessary, as Andy has already done that masterfully.[261] Besides, refuting the crux of the story is not the point to be made here.

For our purposes, the most relevant observation is that the story was purchased and paid for by one of those outside forces attempting to reshape the food system. In Andy's words: "The money for the story came from an $886,600 grant to the *Guardian* expressly to sponsor and publish anti-livestock stories from an animal-liberation program that is under an entity with a pleasant, nondescript name, 'Open Philanthropy Project.'"[262]

Let's unpack that.

This incident involved two newspapers: the capital-city newspaper and the newspaper for the state's largest city, the *Raleigh News & Observer* and the *Charlotte Observer*, respectively, in the ninth most populous state in the United States. North Carolina's pork industry generates more than $10 billion in economic activity and supports more than 44,000 jobs. It ranks third nationally in the total number of hogs and pigs produced. It is home to the largest pork-processing facility in the world, for now.

The story itself was written by a freelance writer whose work was funded by an advocacy organization. That advocacy organization opposes animal agriculture. And, in the most charitable description possible, the story that was cooked up here woefully misled its readers.

Once again, in Andy's words:

---

260. If anything, the lack of impromptu complaint-driven inspections is a strength of the state's regulatory regime, not a sign of its weakness.

261. "Latest attack by N&O is false, harmful," News, NC Pork Council, last modified September 16, 2019, *https://www.ncpork.org/latest-attack-false-harmful/*.

262. *Ibid.*

> *The story is inaccurate on three counts:*
>
> *It gets facts wrong.*
>
> *It leaves out crucial information.*
>
> *It is funded directly by an advocacy influence campaign, which was not disclosed.*
>
> *It is also part of a dangerous trend: advocacy disguised as journalism, bought and paid with hundreds of thousands of dollars to support stories that amplify a policy agenda against raising livestock for food.*

The authors purported to be the "good guys," looking out for truth and justice, hoping to educate the public on the paucity of oversight of hog farms. They were purportedly presenting objective data. In this case, that data related to environmental complaints at hog farms and the state's response to those.[263] In a state with a unique annual inspection process, outside complaints were more rare, but that certainly did not mean those facilities were not the subject of government oversight and scrutiny. What the authors produced, in cherry-picking what data to share and what to conceal, made for a bogus storyline. Pure fanaticism. Fake news.

Save your anger and indignation. Instead, think for a moment about how this happened.

A fledgling newspaper, always hungry for a story someone might read beyond the first paragraph—or more accurately hover over and click—relied on an outside group to supply content for the front page of the Sunday edition. In some ways, one could view the newspaper the same way some foodies view the farmer, suggesting they are so powerless we shouldn't even hold their negligence against them.

263. The corruption in this particular article was the sleight of hand that suggested our state's hog farms—which required vigorous annual inspection—were less regulated than those states that had an inspection system largely based on responding to complaints. A complaint-driven regime would obviously produce more complaints, particularly if it did not accompany a mandatory, annual inspection program.

Regardless of who you view as more culpable, the newspaper or the outside organization that financed and planted the story, it is clear there would have been no content to share were it not for the existence of an entity that spends so much of its time thinking about how to completely overhaul modern American agriculture, generating and placing propaganda when necessary.

This story was no accident. Nor was its timing. Or placement. Or the misimpressions it left behind. The Russians might even learn a thing or two from how well this misinformation campaign was conceived and executed.

Fortunately, in this case, Andy fought back. He still had personal relationships with the newspaper and made clear to the decision-makers there that the article should not have met what were—at one time, at least—their journalistic standards. Unfortunately, even if the newspaper reflected on Andy's admonishment and felt some remorse for selling its front page to an anti-animal agriculture advocacy organization, the damage had largely been done. Score another one for the anti-aggies. Ag outsiders, 1. Aggie insiders, 0.

But surely anti-modern agriculture apologists do not have the power to regularly shift public opinion on a topic as broad as the safety, efficacy, and viability of the American food system? Think again.

In 2017, a Harvard University Professor concluded that it did not take placing a big story in the *New York Times* to dramatically influence the national conversation.[264]

> *The answer, says Albert J. Weatherhead III University Professor Gary King, is that in an age that relies on internet publication and social-media dispersal, even small- to medium-size media outlets can have a*

264. Peter Reuell, "Small Media, Big Payback," the *Harvard Gazette,* November 9, 2017, *https://news.harvard.edu/gazette/story/2017/11/small-media-can-have-broad-impact-on-the-national-conversation/.*

> *dramatic impact on the content and partisan balance of the national conversation about major public-policy issues.*

Professor King and his colleagues found that the magic number was three. If just three outlets wrote about a major national policy topic, social media attention to that topic increased by more than 62 percent. This was sufficient to sway the national conversation around that topic by several percentage points.

This means that stories that might otherwise live in a local or small market for only a day or so can, if triangulated carefully, become what appears to be a story of genuine national interest. It seems that the advocacy groups that are gaining ground with their critiques of agriculture are well aware of this capability.

In many ways, the problem is exacerbated by the fact that much of the media world is closely networked and generally pays close attention to its own players. In other words, to itself. The press, for example, has an especially deep fondness for following one another on Twitter.[265] One observer put it this way:

> *Because journalists are hooked on Twitter, they often—no, constantly—write news stories about things that happen on the platform. Our biggest problem is this phenomenon: Something happens on Twitter; celebrities, politicians and journalists talk about it, and it's circulated to a wider audience by Twitter's algorithms; journalists write about the dustup. They often present the subject as a debate roiling the country, when it's really just an argument taking place inside that journalist's Twitter feed.*

265. Benjamin Reilly, "Twitter Is Not as Important as Journalists Make It Seem," the *Atlantic*, February 12, 2020, *https://www.theatlantic.com/letters/archive/2020/02/twitter-is-bad-for-the-news/605782/*.

> *Regular people are left with a confused, agitated view of our current political discourse and in many cases of our fellow Americans.*[266]

As the political consultants like to say: "Twitter is not real life." What I would say back is, "No, but that is the real life many journalists live."

This, of course, is not a new problem. William H. Dutton is an emeritus professor at the University of Southern California (since 2002). He is affiliated with the Oxford Internet Institute as a senior fellow, and the Global Cyber Security Capacity Center of the Department of Computer Science as an Oxford Martin Fellow. Dr. Dutton equates today's digital journalism echo chamber to the concept of "pack journalism," a phrase coined during the Nixon-McGovern election campaigns of 1972. Journalists following the campaigns in that era often hitched a ride—together—on a bus, giving them ample opportunity to compare notes and compare their observations (or, more likely their grumblings, cynicism, and sarcasm—and to be clear, I don't blame them for that) as they prepared their stories. What resulted was the rise of generally uniform reporting on key moments in the campaign, even though human experience would suggest that each individual writer should scrutinize (and summarize and report) those moments differently. The "pack" of reporters not only rode together, they ate, drank, and caroused together day after day, night after night, week after week. Eventually, "all their stories begin to sound the same."[267] Timothy Crouse wrote about this in his famous 1973 book, *The Boys on the Bus*, which is still used in journalism schools across the U.S. today.

In the modern era, the problem persists. According to Professor Dutton, "Despite blogging and Tweets galore, the news is likely to

---

266. *Ibid.*

267. Timothy Crouse, "The Boys on the Bus," *Rolling Stone*, October 12, 1972, *https://www.rollingstone.com/politics/politics-news/the-boys-on-the-bus-172403/*.

present [just] one perspective on a demonstration, as well as most other political events, as journalists are more networked—not just on the bus, but—nationally and globally, than ever before possible." Reporters, it seems, are a bit like dominoes. If you can get the first one to fall, the others are apt to do the same.

Perhaps no person has served as a better counterweight to the media's willingness to reprint misgivings about food and agriculture in America than Jayson Lusk. Dr. Lusk is a distinguished professor and head of the Agricultural Economics Department at Purdue University, a gifted communicator, and a prolific writer. In 2013, he wrote *The Food Police: A Well-Fed Manifesto About the Politics of Your Plate*. He has since released *Unnaturally Delicious: How Science and Technology are Serving Up Super Foods to Save the World*. I commend them both to you.

At its heart, Dr. Lusk's work embodies the opposite of what the ag community generally gets from the popular press. He regularly presents data to support the conclusion that much of what the agricultural system's outside agitators advocate for will, in actuality, make the most vulnerable in society even more food insecure. In my experience, the tradeoffs that society would have to make to adopt much of what is proposed by those who want to transform food are scarcely discussed. As an aside, I think the tradeoffs of almost any national policy are frequently not fully explored or explained. Lusk has been a strong advocate for changing that.

> *I don't think I've ever argued that our current agricultural production system doesn't face challenges, rather one needs to understand the tradeoffs and consequences of attempts to move away from our current system and consider whether the policies*

being proposed will actually create the outcomes people want.[268]

It sure is hard to discuss tradeoffs if you're a media outlet that farms out your front page to anti-modern agriculture advocates.

You may be curious about the triangulation theory, that is, Professor Dutton's research that concludes three is the magic number for boosting a story's visibility. Just how do outside groups hoping to influence thinking (and thus direction) of the future of food and farming debate take advantage of that? A recent spate of stories regarding salmonella, a naturally occurring bacteria that sometimes surfaces in the live or raw poultry supply, provides an eye-opening illustration.

On October 29, 2021, four reporters at ProPublica published a lengthy story with the following opening volley: "For years, a dangerous salmonella strain has sickened thousands and continues to spread through the chicken industry. The USDA knows about it. So do the companies. And yet, contaminated meat continues to be sold to consumers."[269]

There is no mistaking that the purpose of the article was to leave the reader with the impression that a potentially deadly and pervasive form of salmonella runs rampant in the U.S. food supply, and that neither the government nor industry cares anything about it. Never mind that properly handled and prepared poultry poses no risk to society or even to vulnerable populations. And never mind that salmonella outbreak investigations have identified the bacteria in "vegetables, fresh produce, cereals, cantaloupes, alfalfa sprouts, pistachios, fruit/fruit pulp, ground beef and turkeys, . . . pork, tuna,

---

268. "Jayson Lusk Works to Reframe Food Debates with Data," December, Food Tank, last modified December 15, 2017, *https://foodtank.com/news/2017/12/jayson-lusk-interview/.*

269. Bernice Yeung, et al., "America's Food Safety System Failed to Stop a Salmonella Epidemic. It's Still Making People Sick.," *ProPublica,* October 29, 2021, *https://www.propublica.org/article/salmonella-chicken-usda-food-safety.*

dried/shredded coconut, and tomatoes."[270] In fact, scientists who have studied it closely call *Salmonella enterica* "one of the most ubiquitous enteropathogenic bacterial species on earth."

Within mere days after the October 29 story was published on ProPublica's site, it was reprinted in a myriad of other outlets. ProPublica made this easy. In fact, they encouraged it. Any reader could click a button, agree to the terms of a creative commons license, and assuming they included ProPublica's newsletter sign-up solicitation, they were free to use the article. Several did.

WallStreetWindow.[271] Global Biodefense.[272] The Society of Environmental Justice.[273] Even the *Tucson Sentinel*.[274] Medium and Reddit got in on the game, too.[275] To me, the most notable reproduction ran in *Government Executive*'s online portal.[276] In the

270. Divek Nair, Kumar Venkitanarayanan, and Anup Kollanoor Johny, *Antibiotic-Resistant Salmonella in the Food Supply and the Potential Role of Antibiotic Alternatives for Control* (Foods, 2018), MDPI Journals, available at: *https://www.ncbi.nlm.nih.gov/pmc/articles/PMC6210005/*.

271. "America's Food Safety System Failed to Stop a Salmonella Epidemic. It's Still Making People Sick.," US Politics, Wall Street Window, last modified November 2, 2021, *https://wallstreetwindow.com/2021/11/americas-food-safety-system-failed-to-stop-a-salmonella-epidemic-its-still-making-people-sick-bernice-yeung-michael-grabell-irena-hwang-and-mollie-simon/*.

272. Bernice Yeung, et al., "America's Food Safety System Failed to Stop a Salmonella Epidemic. It's Still Making People Sick." *Global BioDefense,* October 29, 2021, *https://globalbiodefense.com/2021/10/29/americas-food-safety-system-failed-to-stop-a-salmonella-epidemic-its-still-making-people-sick/*.

273. "America's Food Safety System Failed to Stop a Salmonella Epidemic," Headlines, Society of Environmental Journalists, last modified November 2, 2021, *https://www.sej.org/headlines/america-s-food-safety-system-failed-stop-salmonella-epidemic*.

274. "Food," Category, *Tucson Sentinel*, last modified November 24, 2021, *http://www.tucsonsentinel.com/category/food/*.

275. Jennifer Geer, "US Regulators Have Failed to Prevent Deadly Salmonella From Circulating in the Food Supply," Medium, November 3, 2021, *https://medium.com/exploring-wellness/us-regulators-have-failed-to-prevent-deadly-salmonella-from-circulating-in-the-food-supply-fe971e61c9d1*. And Mako (@u/mako_anomaly), "ProPublica on Salmonella in the US Poultry Supply," Reddit, November 11, 2021, *https://www.reddit.com/r/healthinspector/comments/qla36e/propublica_on_salmonella_in_the_us_poultry_supply/*.

276. Bernice Yeung, et al., "America's Food Safety System Failed to Stop a Salmonella Epidemic. It's Still Making People Sick.," *Government Executive,* October 31, 2021,

event you're not an avid reader, here's what you need to know about *Government Executive*:

> *Government Executive is government's business news daily and the premier digital destination for senior leaders in the federal government's departments and agencies. Our readers are the high-ranking civilian and military officials who are responsible for defending the nation and carrying out the laws that define the government's role in our economy and society.*[277]

In other words, *Government Executive* claims it is the E. F. Hutton of those protecting us at the highest levels of government. And it just sent them all an article that was designed to convince them that the poultry-processing system in America is broken.

Some publications wrote their own version of the story, including MedPage Today.[278] By the time you read this, I'm sure there have been dozens more.

Add all of this together and it means the following: the next time you search for information on salmonella, you will find numerous articles lamenting its unchecked spread in the chicken world. You will be slapped in the face with the impression that the poultry supply chain is extremely compromised, that government is impotent to investigate it, and that the poultry industry is ignoring it or is indifferent to it. Never mind that none of that is true.

---

https://www.govexec.com/oversight/2021/10/americas-food-safety-system-failed-stop-salmonella-epidemic-its-still-making-people-sick/186481/.

277. "About Government Executive," About, Government Executive, last modified December 1, 2021, *https://www.govexec.com/about/?oref=ge-nav.*

278. Jennifer Henderson, "Dangerous Bacteria Circulating; Disinfo Docs Go Unpunished; Enbrel's Patent Thicket," MedPage Today, November 3, 2021, *https://www.medpagetoday.com/special-reports/exclusives/95417.*

The practice of building an echo chamber media narrative by pushing the same content out to multiple sites and publications is not the only way advocacy-oriented messaging is distributed. In other instances, smaller organizations that refer to themselves as news or journalism outlets partner with a larger media outlet to push their narrative. These partnerships are sometimes disclosed to readers as "collaborations." The situation described at the outset of this chapter is an example. But there are others.

Two writers for Grist, Nathanael Johnson and Ysabelle Kempe, recently published a piece entitled "The US Is About to Go All-in on Paying Farmers and Foresters to Trap Carbon."[279] This article was released in July of 2021, just as policy conversations regarding incentives for carbon offsets were hitting their stride. The subhead of the article read, "The problem is, it's unclear if 'carbon offsets' even work." It is not hard to understand the gist of the writers' story:

> *Since signing up with Nori, [a farmer featured in the story with the last name] Garrett has raked in nearly $150,000 for capturing carbon in his soil, though it's hard to know exactly how much carbon Garrett is actually storing. And because of that, it's impossible to know if he's storing more carbon than he would have put into his fields if he hadn't gotten paid. That's a problem for the carbon offset market (which is somewhere around a billion dollars according to some reports), which is built on the idea that money will persuade someone, somewhere, to remove additional carbon dioxide from the air.*

279. Nathanael Johnson and Ysabelle Kempe, "The US is about to go all-in on paying farmers and foresters to trap carbon," *Grist*, July 7, 2021, *https://grist.org/agriculture/us-carbon-removal-capture-offset-forests-farms-trees-soil/*.

In fairness, the authors make some good points about knowing the fine particulars of just how effective carbon-capture programs and incentives are or will be. For our purposes, the point here is to read the fine print.

One day after the Grist piece went live, it appeared on *Rolling Stone*'s site. The headline and subhead were identical to Grist's.[280] A one sentence disclaimer appears at the outset of the article: "This story was originally published by Grist and is republished here as part of an ongoing collaboration." An ongoing collaboration? So *Rolling Stone*, which describes itself as an American monthly magazine that focuses on music, politics, and popular culture, is collaborating with Grist, which describes itself as "a nonprofit, independent media organization dedicated to telling stories of climate solutions and a just future." Good to know. In fact, Grist prides itself on this kind of collaboration. In their 2018 form 990, they specifically mention that part of their mission is "serving as a resource for other media," including serving as "an expert source."[281] In their words, "Across the country, journalists and other influencers turn to Grist for enlightenment and elaboration." And you thought enlightenment was so 1700s.

But these "collaborations" are common.

FERN, the Food & Environment Reporting Network, has spawned many of them over the years.[282] In fact, that's the point. It is, after all, a "reporting network." It describes its unbiased view of the modern American food system as follows:

---

280. Nathanael Johnson and Ysabelle Kempe, "The U.S. Is About to Go All in on Paying Farmers and Foresters to Trap Carbon," *Rolling Stone*, July 8, 2021, *https://www.rollingstone.com/politics/politics-features/the-u-s-is-about-to-go-all-in-on-paying-farmers-and-foresters-to-trap-carbon-1194250/*.

281. Department of the Treasury Internal Revenue Service, *Return of Organization Exempt From Income Tax* (Washington: Grist Magazine Inc., 2018), Public Disclosure Copy, *available at*: *https://drive.google.com/file/d/178HmgNXFaLYCD4-02bn3CiOaZo32zkRs/view*.

282. "Tracking Our Impact," About, The Food & Environment Reporting Network, last modified November 18, 2021, *https://thefern.org/impact/*.

> *Through our impartial "watchdog" journalism we seek to shine a light on injustices and abuses of power within the food system—both corporate and governmental—while taking full measure of the true impact food and agriculture have on people, public health, animals, and the environment.*[283]

Injustices? Abuses of power? True impact? Wow. Sounds just like "impartial 'watchdog' journalism"!

In FERN's view, having advocacy organizations write pieces that are then distributed through real journalism outlets is the new model of journalism.

> *New media has challenged the old model of journalism and has opened opportunities to spread stories far beyond their original publication. We believe the future of media will require partnerships between non-profit and for-profit outlets to produce these costly and yet absolutely critical stories and to provide communications support after publication.*[284]

It gets better. Not only do organizations like FERN work to place their advocacy pieces in more mainstream publications, they also develop and deploy the journalists they've trained within their organizations to graduate into more mainstream publications as reporters. Most recently, a writer for FERN took a role with Reuters. Watch out for more stories on the injustices and abuses of power within the food system. In an "impartial watchdog" sort of way, of course.

FERN has also launched an Ag Insider policy news service. They are targeting what they call a "small but influential audience

283. "What We Do," About, The Food & Environment Reporting Network, last modified November 18, 2021, *https://thefern.org/what-we-do/*.

284. *Ibid.*

of policymakers, government officials, advocates, and food industry representatives." There's a free e-mail version and a more in-depth subscription package. According to FERN's 2020 Annual Report, "we now have several hundred individual and corporate subscribers and a growing number of academic institutional subscribers, including New York University, Harvard Law School, University of California, Berkeley, Tufts, Yale, and the University of Pennsylvania."[285] I don't believe the farm community's newsletters are experiencing the same level of uptake, at least not in those venues.

Grist makes no bones about their efforts to train up the next generation of journalists: "By providing hands-on journalism experience as well as exposure to leading environmental thinkers, the Grist Fellowship program trains early-career journalists to become effective environmental communicators."[286]

At the venerable University of California at Berkeley Graduate School of Journalism, one might think they could bring a farming perspective to the table by applying for an "11th Hour Food and Farming Journalism Fellowship."[287] Given that Michael Pollan is a professor there, it should come as no surprise that neither of the most recent classes of fellows included even one rural resident. I guess we can look forward to more agricultural and food system journalism written by people who live in New York City.

I've mentioned the *Guardian*, Grist, and FERN. But there's also Food & Power. The Counter, which used to be the New Food Economy. Civil Eats. Vox's Future Perfect. The Open Markets Fair

285. Fern News, *2020 Annual Report* (Food & Environment Reporting Network, 2020), Fern News, available at: *https://fernnews-wpengine.netdna-ssl.com/wp-content/uploads/2021/03/FERN-Annual-Report-2020.pdf.*

286. Department of the Treasury Internal Revenue Service, *Return of Organization Exempt From Income Tax* (Washington: Grist Magazine Inc., 2018), Public Disclosure Copy, *available at: https://drive.google.com/file/d/178HmgNXFaLYCD4-02bn3CiOaZo32zkRs/view.*

287. Berkeley Journalism, *The UC Berkeley - 11th Hour Food and Farming Journalism Fellowship*, available at: *https://projects.journalism.berkeley.edu/foodfellows/.*

Food & Farming Systems program. Friends of the Earth. And I could go on. The natural question here is whether anybody is preparing to counter this offensive? In other words, who is bringing the perspective held by the millions who do not believe the food system is inherently unjust and abusive? Or who believe that the greatest impact of the food and agriculture system in the United States has primarily been the flourishing of innovation across other sectors and access to the safest, most affordable food supply of any venue in the world? My concern is that those questions remained unanswered. Left unanswered long enough, the imbalance in the journalistic narrative will, I fear, erode trust in farmers and our food system among the general populace.

On that note, let's go back to Andy and the statewide Sunday newspapers. Recall that the article described at the outset of this chapter was not the work of disinterested investigative reporters. It was blatantly biased. And it was blatantly biased because it was meant to be biased. In this instance, it was the media machine that was broken, which allowed the ag outsiders to use it for their purposes. Today, the increasingly dominant narrative is that the same system that has given us so much over the years, and which shows so much promise as we enter the "food as medicine" era, now needs quantum leaps and organ transplants to be made right.

Some of the articles and quotes captured above are like the one Andy swiftly disassembled. Openly biased and self-serving.

But they make for good clickbait. Someone else will quote them in yet another article. Or in a paper for a class. Or in a book. Tracing the roots of these stories or the motivations of each of their authors is not my goal, nor would it further illustrate the point. The point is that these views exist, they are held by widely influential members of our society, they are not going away on their own, and at the moment, at least, there is no credible counterweight to them in the sprawling media sphere. Industry efforts to push back are dismissed as biased. The agriculture community's response often turns inward. And we wonder why people hold the views they do.

I guess investigative reporting just isn't what it used to be. What agriculture—and society—needs, are folks who are smart, nimble and who have new media sensibility rooted in the foundations of journalism as it should be practiced.

CHAPTER ELEVEN

Getting a Little Agri-Culture

Have you ever contemplated doing something entirely different as a career? I remember a fellow law student and I discussing what restaurant we would open when we dropped out of school.[288] There was a time I wanted to own and operate a gym.[289] I still think I would have been a pretty good ag teacher and eventually a decent principal, which was the plan until about halfway through college. "I should

288. We ultimately came to the conclusion that the only one we could afford was a Subway. My friend Barry researched what was required to establish such a franchise and concluded you needed "$5,000 and a box of envelopes." To this day, I look enviously on the meatball sub and think about how I could have eaten thousands of them by now if Barry had just ponied up $5,000 and I had possessed an unopened box of envelopes.

289. If you were to meet me, you would have no trouble believing I could spend more time in one.

have done the MBA, or maybe the joint MBA and law degree," I've lectured myself. The ministry, military service, or a deeper dive into economics have all seemed, at one time or another, like attractive alternatives. Yet as I've aged, one field of study rises to the top of the "I should have" list more consistently than the others: anthropology.

From the homepage of the American Anthropological Association:

> *From the Greek anthropos (human) and logia (study), the word anthropology itself tells us it is the field that seeks to understand humankind, from the beginnings millions of years ago up to the present day. Anthropology considers how people's behaviors change over time, and how people and seemingly dissimilar cultures are different and the same.*[290]

The promise of better understanding humankind, and thus why humans make the decisions they do, is intoxicatingly tempting for me, but it should also be tempting for folks hoping to better understand the mindset of foodies and other food system outsiders. Being able to explain why people buy anything that has been "unicorned" or have a desire to avocado things that are perfectly good without it (or with butter) could possibly restore my faith in the human race. Or make it deteriorate further. More relevant to the crux of this book, a valid question would be why so many Americans share an idyllic view of farms while at the same time they are seemingly predisposed to like them less the more food they produce?

I share the anthropologists' desire to know what people think is important, and to better understand why they think that what they think is important, particularly their thoughts and opinions about

290. "What do Anthropologists do?," Advance Your Career, American Anthropological Association, last modified November 17, 2021, *https://www.americananthro.org/AdvanceYourCareer/Content.aspx?ItemNumber=2148.*

farming and food production. Chances are that you've asked yourself some of these same questions.

There are many funny stories about how culture works. They are even more humorous when they involve public policy efforts that fail to account for culture's importance. For example, in Singapore, a tax designed to make vehicles more expensive, and thus to encourage the use of public transportation, ultimately backfired. The authors of a study concluded that Singaporeans, even ecologically aware ones, shared a view that "those who drive are smarter, more educated, and higher class."[291] As a result, the tax that made driving more expensive ultimately reinforced that view, because driving became an even greater symbol of wealth. Needless to say, the tax ultimately discouraged the use of public transportation.

It is not, however, just governments that must attend to the forces of culture. For those of us who want to better understand the minds of food system outsiders, and to potentially influence them, we must have some awareness of the culture in which those minds are shaped. In the words of Dr. Ruth Fulton Benedict, a former president of the American Anthropological Association and the first woman to be regarded as a prominent leader of a learned profession, "The crucial differences which distinguish human societies and human beings are not biological. They are cultural."

As an aside, us aggies have our own cultural proclivities, too. We often don't see them until somebody outside the family points them out. I had one such experience just a couple of years ago. While living in Northern Virginia and working in Washington, my family and I brought a friend of ours to the family farm I grew up on in Southeast North Carolina. This friend, Julie, had never been on a farm. She was, like my wife, an accomplished math teacher, not an agrarian. She could run circles around the best tour guides of New

291. Kim Armstrong, "The WEIRD Science of Culture, Values, and Behavior," Association for Psychological Science, March 30, 2018, *https://www.psychologicalscience.org/observer/the-weird-science-of-culture-values-and-behavior*.

York City, but she had never ridden in a pick-up truck. Anywhere. Much less a combine, which she had the opportunity to do during her trip to Starling Farms. Julie had lots of questions about how things worked, why things were done the way they were, and what we called different things down on the farm. She might have ordinarily been a splendid teacher, but on this day she and our other agritourism guests were splendid students. My brother Willi was their teacher.

It was Julie that challenged me in a way I had not expected. Namely, by asking a simple question: "Why do you pronounce 'combine' the way you do?"

Stop, like I did, and think for a moment about the word "combine." For everyone involved in agriculture, we view that word, at least when it is used in the farm context, as COM-bine. For everyone else, including Julie, it is pronounced cum-BINE.

This is even more vexing when you consider that the common name for this machine came from the fact that it merges—or combines—several different functions required to harvest within one apparatus. "Reaping, threshing, winnowing—combining all three operations into one led to the invention of the combine harvester, simply known as the combine."[292] In fact, I could find no convincing explanation for why those of us in agriculture have created an entirely new pronunciation for this word. But we have. To pronounce it differently amongst a group of aggies would engender glances and looks typically reserved for vegetarians at a Pig Jig.

As Julie helped me understand, those of us in agriculture sometimes do not even realize that we are really functioning within a subculture, with a system of meaning and shared beliefs that may or may not align with our larger society. Most aggies have

292. Mary Herring, in a May 2020 piece entitled "A Brief History of the Combine," offers a succinct and enthralling history of the combine. I would be the first to admit that I found reading her piece more interesting than writing this one. Mary Herring, "Harvest Equipment: A Brief History of the Combine," *Iron Solutions,* May 24, 2020, *https://ironsolutions.com/agriculture-equipment-value-guides/a-brief-history-of-the-combine/.*

a fondness for the "blue and gold," or have pledged their "hands to larger service." There are few things more entertaining than hearing farmers who are otherwise complete strangers talk, well... farming. An immediate bond is present. A shared kinsmanship. A family reunion, but with people you do not recognize. There are shared frustrations ("Why does the sensor mechanism cost more than the thing the sensor was supposed to sense?") and shared joys ("It started raining just as we got her into the shelter").

Is it possible, then, that there are cultural forces outside of the agriculture community that are shaping how people think about agricultural insiders and the work they do? Might some of the insider-outsider disconnects chronicled in this book be explained by upstream cultural forces that have reframed what many of our non-ag brethren believe they can expect from the farming and food ecosystem? More interestingly, could some of those cultural norms be shaping us, even if we don't recognize them? Your author has already admitted he is no cultural anthropologist, but refuting that the modern-day farming and food system critic brings cultural baggage to their assessment of the food and fiber enterprise seems like a dumb hill to die on. In other words, yes, there are changing cultural norms that help explain outsiders' views and why they may be different today than they were just a few decades ago.

So what are those changing cultural norms, and how do they help explain the Humpty Dumptyism aimed at the agricultural community? I will cover three. The first is the continual rise in individualism. The second is society's shift to a consumption mindset as opposed to a production one. And the third is our continual quest to find purpose, which may afflict the farm community as much as it does the general population, but in different ways.

Individualism and Expressive Individualism

Individualism and individualist culture are generally terms used to describe a person or people who prize independence and uniqueness as cultural values. Contrast the strong American preference for this perspective with that of our friends in East Asia, who are more likely to "foster an interdependent self-construal, with a self that is more relational, harmonious, and interconnected with others."[293] In that context, interdependence is stressed over independence. In ours, the heroes are increasingly not ones that sacrifice for the greater good of their community, but who "find themselves" by looking inwardly. In doing so, they achieve their "true selves." It is not uncommon to see these two opposites juxtaposed as individualism versus collectivism.

Closely aligned with this individualism is a new emphasis on expressing it, sometimes called expressive individualism.[294] The phrases "you do you," and "to each her own," come to mind. In today's society, we seem to have strong debates over objective truth, frequently consoling one another that something was "true to you," or that it was "your truth." We might even encourage someone by saying, "Live your truth," "Discover your true self," or "Do your own thing." Or, to borrow from the Isley Brothers' 1969 hit "It's Your Thing": "Do what you wanna do." Consider the allure of a "choose your own adventure" escapade. And sadly, choose your own facts.

What does any of this have to do with how people think of food and farming? My sense is that it is at least one explanation for how

293. Marianna Pogosyan, "How Culture Wires Our Brains: Cultural values may leave a greater impact on our brain more than our behaviors." January 26, 2017. https://www.psychologytoday.com/us/blog/between-cultures/201701/how-culture-wires-our-brains

294. Robert Bellah and a team of researchers wrote extensively about this cultural phenomena in their book *Habits of the Heart*, first published in 1985. I can do that body of research no justice here, but am referring to it merely to make the point that I believe the same brand of individualism that Bellah believed threatened our democratic institutions also influences Americans' impressions of the modern farm and food enterprises.

someone in the United States—with access to a food system that allows them to spend a lower portion of their income on food than any other country in the world, and to which is owed the many other superlatives repeated often in these pages—can nonetheless conclude the food system is broken. By any objective measure, this is patently absurd. If anything, the complaint that we are "too good" at producing food is more believable than the complaint that the system is broken. Yet if we are in a society that values everyone's subjective truths over actual truth, those beliefs can remain unchallenged.

To go a step further, because those beliefs run counter to the more common, correct beliefs, they are given elevated status. They are sometimes couched as "speaking out against corporate agriculture," or in a more general sense "speaking truth to power." People that espouse them win awards and secure interviews in publications read by the elite. They do TED Talks. Write books. The myths they promote become truths that only the enlightened are capable of holding. The rest of us dufuses just don't get it. In short, an extension of this characteristic of our modern culture—this emphasis on individualism—is that it allows for the bold repetition of claims that are not grounded in fact and that are all the more likely to be adopted and repeated by a public that knows less and less about agriculture and farming.

Some scholars maintain that individualism flourishes in societies of plenty. One body of research concluded that the strongest predictor of increased individualism was increased socioeconomic development. "Various aspects of development were related to increases in individualism, particularly increases in the proportion of white-collar jobs, in education levels, and in household income."[295] This is, upon reflection, a perfectly sensible

295. "Individualistic Practices and Values Increasing Around the World," Latest Research News, Psychological Science, last modified July 17, 2017, *https://www.psychologicalscience.org/news/releases/individualistic-practices-and-values-increasing-around-the-world.html.*

conclusion, and it is readily applicable to impressions about food and farming. Remember the quote from Secretary Perdue? "When man has no food, he has one problem, and when he has plenty he has plenty of problems." Critiques of the food system in societies that are food insecure are far, far different from those we hear in a country roundly regarded as the world's economic superpower.

When Burger King promised to let their customers "Have It Your Way," they were tempting them in a way that members of truly food insecure societies could only dream of. But that slogan wasn't good enough for the 2010s. Burger King updated its slogan in 2014 to "Be Your Way." In doing so, they sought to remind people that "they can and should live how they want anytime."[296] Sound like individualism much?

The Canadian philosopher and theologian Charles Taylor wrote extensively about our march toward individualism in *A Secular Age*. Taylor was clearly troubled by the trend, and he cited numerous ills it could likely produce in greater society.[297] While I doubt Taylor specifically contemplated the challenges that the ascension of this cultural mindset would present to the food system or to any debate about what that food system should be, there are nonetheless some lessons for us as we consider his observations.

One of those is that when economic conditions allow for greater individualistic choice, familiarity with shared sacrifice and mutual burden-bearing seem to naturally decline. Many who critique today's system want to live in Burger King land. They want it their way. But they also simultaneously want you to have it their way or don't seem to care if some cannot afford to have it their way. If their way

296. "Burger King scrapping 'Have It Your Way' Slogan," Food & Beverage, CNBC, last modified May 19, 2021, *https://www.cnbc.com/2014/05/19/burger-king-scrapping-have-it-your-way-slogan.html*.

297. You would be better served by listening to Tim Keller or James K. A. Smith discuss Taylor's theories than by listening to me, and I might have completely misinterpreted all three of these gentlemen here. To the extent that I have misrepresented any of them, I do so completely unintentionally.

decreases the availability of food, or increases its cost, that is just a tradeoff that we all need to make, not just one that they need to make. Such an egoistic attitude toward our fellow members of society ignores the fact that the food system doesn't just provide food for each one of us, it has to provide food for *all* of us. Every day.

For anyone who ignores that need, whether ignorantly or purposefully, they are living out one of the risks of hyper-individualism that Taylor was concerned about. Namely, that a rise in individualistic culture corresponds with a decline in "modes of mutual help." In other words, a very good case can be made that many of the reforms brought forward by aggie system outsiders mainly satisfy the egos of those who are privileged enough to call for them, but they potentially annihilate the greater, bigger load carried by that same food system.

CONSUMPTION VERSUS PRODUCTION

Taylor also believed that the rise of individualism went hand in hand with the rise of a consumption mindset. Regarding our society's shift to consumption and its increasing unfamiliarity with production, there is debate about how we got here. Some economists and historians posit that the business community, and corporations in general, started it when they educated the populace about the skill of, or as one economist put it, the "gospel of," consumption.[298] Others argue that as production techniques became more efficient, more and more product could naturally be produced, and ever-increasing natural aspirations could be satisfied. Taylor himself might tell us that postwar affluence brought on a new paradigm of private space (and potentially private time), which resulted in a clamoring to fill it. With things. Whether the aspiration for things was a natural human

298. Kerryn Higgs, "How the World Embraced Consumerism," BBC, January 20, 2021, *https://www.bbc.com/future/article/20210120-how-the-world-became-consumerist.*

tendency—a natural love of stuff—or the product of increased advertising budgets and the suggestion that satisfaction could be found in the next catalog, department store trip, or click, there is no denying the modern-day American has more experience with consumption than production. Bring on the things. All the things.

Many years ago, while rummaging through my Granny and Papa's old house, my brother Steve found a large mason jar containing several soap slivers. These were the leftovers. But they were not going to be thrown away. They were going to be recombined and ultimately used, but Granny and Papa passed on before they ever got around to it. Steve kept the mason jar partly because it reminded him of the frugality of our ancestors. I think he also kept it because it reminded him of just how different our society is today. Why on earth would anyone keep old soap slivers and melt them back into a bar anymore? Today, there are entire stores devoted to selling fragrant soaps and body washes—and to this day I'm not sure I even know the difference. Consumption gumption.

When I wrote a eulogy for my MawMaw-in-law, my wife's grandmother, I remarked about the fact that in her mind, twist ties from bread bags were as precious as coins themselves. It was no exaggeration. I still have a bag of several dozen Ms. Velma was saving and never got the chance to use. You might get the idea that Steve and I believe the grandparents in our lives were on to something.

In my mind, there are at least two reasons why the now culturally dominant consumption mindset is important to understand for those who seek to explore the outside forces shaping the future of farming and food. First, there is seemingly no end to the demands our society is prepared to cast on the food system. While at one time consumer activism in the food space focused on addressing economic adulteration or safety, the movements today are more dispersed: "Today there are, for example, movements for slow food, organic food, local food, fair-trade food—even ethical dog food."[299] For those engaged in farming and food production, the door upon which we seem to endlessly knock—that of a market content with what it has already been given—will never be achieved. This is, in essence, the point of consumerism. That the cat will never catch its tail. There is always a new thing to market, hawk, or push.

While this is arguably promising in many ways, for example on the point that those in the farming and food sector who can successfully create the next consumer craze will be rewarded (kudos to the avocado toast progenitors), we will never achieve a perfect balance between what the system provides today and what will be demanded of it tomorrow. In Solomon's words, expecting the consumer community to grow content with what they already have is akin to us "chasing after the wind." Ironically that is true because the consumer is going to keep chasing the wind. And maybe that can sometimes be a good thing.[300] But it certainly creates continued pressure on the food and farming community to satiate the "what's next" mentality.

Second, as presented here at least, the luxury of being able to focus so intently on the consumption of food has left little time to admire its production. We are now well into a generation of consumers who not only did not grow up on farms, but whose parents and grandparents didn't farm either. Add to that the fact that we are one click away from having our latest book, gadget, or trinket delivered tomorrow. As time marches on, it becomes, for an increasing share of our population, more and more tempting to forget the risky, difficult, dirty, and intelligent work that goes into growing, processing,

---

299. Frank Trentmann, "How Humans Became 'Consumers': A History," the *Atlantic,* November 28, 2016, *https://www.theatlantic.com/business/archive/2016/11/how-humans-became-consumers/508700/.*

300. In fact, it is the consumption mindset that some of the most prolific technologies in agriculture have been designed to address. Arctic apples that don't turn brown when exposed to air, for example. Traceability capabilities in the food chain. Pumpkins that make it home from the farm visit, as opposed to being squished on the floor of the bus.

and transporting our food. As our economy continues its shift toward domestic services and foreign goods, our lack of exposure to production—making stuff—leaves us less and less familiar with all that is required to get food to retail outlets and restaurants. The end result? A consumer who knows what they want, and who wants what they want to be holistically good (as in ethically good, recall the "good foodie" discussed previously), but who has no idea what is actually required to produce it and who cannot explain what's unethical about making food more affordable for more people.

I NEED A CAUSE!

The final cultural observation that I suggest is shaping the debate about how we produce food is our modern-day tendency to search for purpose in and for our lives. In *Man's Search for Meaning*, world-renowned psychiatrist and Nazi concentration camp survivor Viktor Frankl called meaning and a perceived purpose of life the primary, intrinsic motivation of mankind: "A man who becomes conscious of the responsibility he bears towards others, or to an unfinished work, will never be able to throw away his life. He knows the 'why' for his existence, and will be able to bear almost any 'how.'" His book has sold over ten million copies.

Austrian medical doctor and psychotherapist Alfred Adler said that it was a natural characteristic of people to strive to accomplish the purpose of their lives. Erik Erikson, the Danish-German-American developmental psychologist and psychoanalyst who coined the phrase "identity crisis," wrote of how a person must integrate what they've done in their life with what they perceive to be the bigger picture of the world around them. Abraham Maslow, of Maslow's hierarchy fame, put physiological needs at the bottom, but he put self-actualization—pretty darn close to the idea that one's life has meaning and purpose—at the top.

Because of my own personal religious beliefs, it is difficult for me to mention this last characteristic of our culture without mentioning that I believe there is only one way to fix it. To borrow crudely from Blaise Pascal, there's only one shape that fills the God-shaped hole in our hearts. That, however, doesn't keep people from trying other things. Like maintaining that the food system is broken and it is part of their life's purpose to fix it.

Interestingly, I believe it is that same tendency that drives farmers to take their roles in society so seriously and to carry them out so proudly. Indeed, it is likely the connection to their duty to supply food to their fellow man that gets them up early and keeps them out late. In either instance, whether we are considering the deeply held beliefs about the food system that are held by an outsider or insider, we seem to have a tendency to tie those beliefs to a greater purpose for living. As such, those beliefs are held more closely than they would otherwise be held. They are more difficult to shake. And that, I believe, is part of the disconnect we experience when we approach ag system outsiders who are convinced that American agriculture is beyond repair, and that it got that way because of evil corporate farms and food companies. Once a belief becomes tantamount to your purpose in life, it's pretty darn hard to abandon.

Surely there are other cultural shifts and pressures that influence the conversation around what we can and should expect from our farms and food system. I'm prepared to admit that some of them can be good. The point here is not to bemoan the present state of society, or to grump that today's food system critics need to get off my lawn. It's merely to make the point that aggies cannot understand—much less answer—the forces that are forging the future of farming and food without understanding some of the cultural characteristics of the society in which those forces are at work.

Each year since 1986, the public affairs staff at my home state Department of Agriculture choose a theme for the state fair. Of all the themes used over the years, there is one that clearly stands out above the rest. In 1991, the theme was "Get a Little Agri-culture." I loved it then and I love it now.

Those of us with ag in our veins have an innate and somewhat inexplicable desire to educate everyone else who does not suffer equally from ag exceptionalism disorder. Ag exceptionalism disorder is my terminology for the feeling that we should talk about how great farming and agriculture are, particularly in America, and that we should talk about it all the time. We want so badly for others to understand just how impressive America's food and fiber systems are. We want them to "get a little agri-culture." We might make more progress on that front if we stepped back and worked harder to understand some of the cultural foundations of their beliefs.

Let's invite a real anthropologist to our next meeting.

CHAPTER TWELVE

THIS PLANE DOESN'T WAIT ON YOU

Flying with the President of the United States has its privileges. No bag check. No taking off your belt or stripping down to your socks. No waddling through security with the present-day anxiety that comes from being separated from your phone and wallet for more than ten seconds. And no mad dash to stand in line to buy overpriced food before you board. Turns out they have food on the plane. (I ended up not needing my pack of nabs.)

While I'm a big fan of the Presidential seal M&M's (although I wish they had the peanut kind), I was most impressed by the real food served on the big bird. Specifically, the chili. The Presidential Airlift Group may be better known for their impeccable maintenance of Air Force One, but they could win a chili cook-off hands down.

And that's coming from a guy who has won a chili cook-off or two. I kept the tiny bottle of Tabasco that came with my serving of chili. Mostly because—like everything on Air Force One—it bore the Presidential seal.

I was fortunate enough to fly with the President three times. Unlike the President and his most senior advisors, staff like me are shuttled to Andrews Air Force Base long before the President arrives. We did not travel via much of an armored brigade. We were shipped off in mundane vans that stop for traffic lights and traffic jams. By design, we are supposed to be in place and ready to go long before the President and his detail arrive. On the commute for the President's trip to Iowa to unveil the findings of the Rural Prosperity Task Force, an unanticipated smooth trip from the White House to Andrews meant that my colleagues and I arrived early enough to press the good graces of the President's flight crew. We asked for a tour. After giving me a quick peek into the President's quarters, the operating room, and the conference room, I asked if there was anything else I needed to know as an inexperienced AF1 passenger. I mainly wanted to make sure I didn't violate some unwritten rule of presidential travel etiquette. After a long pause, the polite but professional service member looked me straight in the eye and responded: "There's only one person this plane waits for. And it's not you."

Even I did not need to hear that warning twice. I got it. And she was right. It was all hurry up and wait until the President's motorcade arrived on the tarmac. My colleagues and I peered through the portholes to see if we could catch a glimpse of the pomp and circumstance. The scope of our vision was limited, so we awaited some signal that the President had made it up the stairs and into the plane. I figured there would be an announcement about turning off our devices or stowing our knapsacks. Not so much. The only signal we got—about two minutes after someone first said he had arrived outside—was the fact that the plane started moving. By the time two more minutes had passed, we were in the air.

Like Air Force One, the future of farming and food does not sit around and wait. Those who are shaping the food system from the outside are rumbling down the runway with an intensity, urgency, and volume that is getting harder and harder to monitor, much less match. If we care as deeply about the farming and food industry as we say, the time is now for us to determine how we are going to preserve it.

So how do we do that? To the extent that this book has established that there is a problem, or to use the words of every motivational speaker, an "opportunity," what should we be doing to address it? What is at stake if we don't?

That's the difficulty of writing a book about an existential problem. At some point, your readers will expect you to proffer a solution. Preferably one that can be easily described with three easy steps. Or in a list of "to dos" that all begin with the same letter. I will spare you that. The stakes in the farmer versus foodies debate are too high, and too serious, for such drivel. What I will offer here is a heartfelt and humble recommendation for action, and one that I believe we—meaning those of us in aggie land—are capable of implementing. Let me begin, though, with what we need to stop doing.

A Pile of Unprocessed Anguish

I hope by now that you've found at least one observation in this book that has made you angry. I hope that some of the techniques the outsiders are using incense you. Frustrate you. Make you, as my good friend and onetime National FFA Alumni President Linda Story would say, "madder than a biting sow." (I've seen one of those up close. It ain't pretty.) You likely have felt that way because you love American agriculture, and you love our farmers, the culture that surrounds them, and the contributions they make to the world. When folks whose plow is a pencil start to shake their finger at those who take perennial risk to give us the most affordable, most reliable, and safest food supply in human history, it is enough to make our blood boil.

Unfortunately for us, anger and righteous indignation is not a strategy. For decades, farm leaders have been exposed to earlier iterations of some of the outside forces I have documented here, and sometimes engaged in sincere discussions about how to counteract them. Those discussions have occasionally yielded meaningful campaigns, but often run off the rails in one of two ways. They are either abandoned after a short period of time and replaced with the next great idea, or they become inward facing and ultimately result in our talking to ourselves. In comparing the periodic campaigns of the farm groups to the sustained, continuous efforts of our detractors, I've always referred to the agriculturalists as the wave and our detractors as the undertow. We make some splashes and occasionally knock a few folks down, but the undertow continues to eat away at the shoreline, often unseen until the damage is already done.

Add to that the observation that there is nothing as satisfying to a group of aggies as hearing people who already agree with them say things they agree with more eloquently, preferably at some place where a free meal is involved. For too long, it has been in vogue to gather around the farmer organization microphone and use personal insults and character attacks to belittle those poking and prodding at our industry. We wanted to be as loud as we perceived they were. That probably makes us feel good. But it is a temporary good feeling. And that is precisely why I've tried to do very little of that in this book. I'm just not sure "we will show them," or "man, are they stupid" responses have been effective in stemming the tide of their critiques. In fact, I would suggest that when we respond in those ways, we cede the high ground and conveniently avoid any adult conversation with our detractors.

Another go-to play in our bag of tricks is to launch a communications campaign. We launch initiative after initiative that ends with us promoting ourselves on Facebook. And we dutifully send it to our friends and check back for likes and cross-posts. In the meantime, those who believe the system is broken have raised another million and placed another story in the *Guardian*, got invited to a chat with NPR, released a TikTok, and given the commencement address at a non-ag university.

There is a better way. Unless you think division is a way to success, which clearly many in our political world do at the moment, we have collaborative work to do. There are bound to be some who are critics for now, but who are also allies in waiting. We may just discover that we can work with them if we engage them the way we wish they would engage with us. We would be stronger if we did that together.

Moreover, we have to be more strategic in our outreach. We have to engage in influencer marketing, but not aim it solely at consumers and politicians. It must be aimed at the community that sets curriculum, deploys capital, stands in pulpits, sets international rules of order, and polices legal liability. Our story is compelling. We are on the right side. All we are missing is the "strategery."

Unlike the ag reform crusaders, who mostly want other people to change, we must ask for change from ourselves. There are no quick fixes to securing ourselves from the threats discussed in these pages, and nobody else is going to do it for us. As the very bad meeting detailed in Chapter 1 revealed, we cannot contract out our defense, nor should we want to. We have to order our response, impose a discipline on ourselves to carry it out, and consistently monitor our progress. We have to process our frustrations and turn them into action.

ADMITTING WE HAVE A PROBLEM

First and foremost, we have to admit we have a problem. Which is exactly what I had to do in my own personal life over fifteen years ago.

In 2006, I purchased a 1976 Ford F100, a three-on-the-tree long-bed pick-up, sight unseen, off eBay. It was $1,500. The seller was from Tennessee and offered to meet me halfway between Raleigh and his hometown to trade the truck for my cash. To me, this was a relatively comforting gesture. If the seller was willing to take the risk of driving it the first 150 miles, it must be a decently reliable vehicle. As far as $1,500 trucks go, at least.

I loved it. There was a lot wrong with it, but I didn't care. I had always wanted an old truck. My wife, on the other hand, hated it. She never learned to appreciate the blue smog it left behind, the on-top-of-the-world feeling I got when I shifted from second into third, or the wood block that I learned to use as a tire chock since the emergency break didn't work. (I put a rope on the block so that I could pull it into the cab of the truck without exiting the vehicle. You can use that idea if you have an old truck. Free tip. No charge.)

Unfortunately for me, it wasn't long before I realized I was in over my head. I am not much of a mechanic, and I did not progress very quickly in my efforts to become one. The mechanics I did know loved the thing, but not because they appreciated the craftsmanship of an old Ford. I eventually figured out it was because it was paying for their kids' educations. And their vacations. And their boat(s). After about a year, I agreed to let it go. For $1,500. (So technically, I broke even.) I watched it roll out of the driveway for the last time—through a blue haze—with a wistful tear in my eye. Today, I live out my old truck ownership dreams by riding with my brother Steve in his 1974 Ford F100. I hear his mechanic just got a new boat. It's his second.

Just as I hated to part with my truck, those of us in agriculture hate to part with any of our views about how the industry is going to look in the future or that our critics may be gaining ground. More relevant here, we hate to admit that as the farming population declines and many Americans are further and further removed from our system of production agriculture, the ag system outsiders' competitive advantage in the marketplace of ideas will increase.

In these pages, I have attempted to demonstrate that the arguments that outsiders make about the modern farming and food system are not casual matters to them. They are feverishly leveraging institutions in society—from academia to the private equity markets—to paint the picture of the future of agriculture differently. From my perspective, there is an audience that appears to be predisposed to buy into the hype. Because the outsiders frequently rely on disinformation, misinformation, and incomplete information, they are shaping the jury pool—literally—more successfully than they could have just a couple of decades ago. In the paraphrased words of my favorite law professor, it is hard to argue with people who know less than you do about a topic. You can only draw so much from your knowledge, but your opponent can draw infinitely from an entire world of ignorance.

In speaking with hundreds of people to get their thoughts on the thesis set forth in this book, I did occasionally run into people who disagreed with the premise. One suggested that the market would work all of this out. Another said they had heard this kind of warning before and never saw the threats materialize. Still others fall back to that oft-repeated phrase: "We just need to tell our story." I wish I could agree. But I can't. The facts presented here are, at least to me, far too compelling to ignore. We start by admitting we have a problem.

MAINTAIN THE HIGH GROUND

Second, we must maintain our integrity.

Any senior lawyer will tell you there is an art to preparing a witness for a deposition or trial testimony. When I was in private practice, I had a trusted process for witness preparation that included giving the witness a barely legible Xerox copy of an old American Bar Association article with tips on how to put their best foot forward. During preparation, the witness always seemed to know the most sensitive parts of their testimony and would inevitably ask what to say if they were asked a certain question. In my role as an officer of the court and an advocate, my response always began with "tell the truth."

For American agriculture insiders, this is typically not difficult to do. Many of the most watched statistics that track our progress tell a mesmerizing story. For example:

1. The level of U.S. farm output nearly tripled between 1948 and 2017, growing at an average annual rate of 1.53 percent.[301]
2. This output was achieved even though labor and land use in agriculture declined.[302] In fact, farmers and ranchers have reduced their labor use by 75 percent and land use by 24 percent.[303]

301. Njuki, Eric. "A Look at Agricultural Productivity Growth in the United States, 1948–2017." USDA blog. United States Department of Agriculture. July 29, 2021. *https://www.usda.gov/media/blog/2020/03/05/look-agricultural-productivity-growth-united-states-1948-2017.*

302. *Ibid.*

303. "USA: A Powerful Legacy with Room to Grow," Virginia Tech GAP Report Initiative, last modified October 16, 2018, *https://globalagriculturalproductivity.org/sustainable-food-and-agriculture-systems-are-built-on-productivity/regional-productivity-growth-progress-and-challenges/usa-a-productivity-powerhouse-loses-some-steam/.*

3. U.S. agriculture and food sectors are key drivers of economic growth, producing $2 trillion in annual revenue and $130 billion in profit for more than 2.6 million businesses.[304]
4. In 1900, it took 37.9 percent of the national labor force to feed and clothe 76 million U.S. consumers, a consumer-to-farmer ratio of 13:1. By 2017, the number of U.S. consumers had grown to 325 million, and the farm labor force had dropped to 1.1 percent of the national total. Thus the current consumer-to-farmer ration is 159:1 and growing.[305]
5. In 2018, $139.6 billion worth of American agricultural products were exported around the world. The United States sells more food and fiber to world markets than we import, creating a positive agricultural trade balance.[306]

I could go on. Mac Davis's 1980 hit song containing the phrase "Oh Lord it's hard to be humble, when you're perfect in every way" comes to mind. Our farmers have produced a bounty that would boggle the minds of people living just one hundred years ago. The men and women who drive our tractors and work our livestock have freed up a larger part of society to pursue other work. And the work is hard. Of the many admirations I have for my parents, few surpass my respect for their work ethic and what they have contributed to society as farmers. With all the good there is to brag about, it puzzles me that we are sometimes tempted to paint the picture a little rosier than it really is.

Some of the people who read the forthcoming critique of a few of our most famous talking points will be upset. Others will suggest

304. *Ibid.*

305. Philip G. Pardey and Julian M. Alston, "The Drivers of U.S. Agricultural Productivity Growth," Federal Reserve Bank of Kansas City, (n.d.) available *https://www.kansascityfed.org/documents/7107/the-drivers-of-us-agricultural-productivity-growth.pdf.*

306. "Fast Facts about Agriculture and Food," American Farm Bureau, (n.d.), *https://www.fb.org/newsroom/fast-facts.*

my ideas are heretical. Or stupid. Still others will question why I felt like this information needed to be included here, or mentioned at all. Well, my intention is to tell the truth. And the truth is that some of the arguments we use to promote American agriculture deserve a little more discussion.

There's the old adage that "American farmers feed the world." There's no debating that we add to the global buffet, but that buffet is quite large. America's contribution has never flirted with more than 10 percent global output. While we are the most generous nation in the world, particularly when it comes to efforts to end malnourishment, it is not our annual harvests that have had the most lasting impact. It is our ingenuity. Our innovation. The intellectual property conceived, developed, tested, and deployed here first, and then exported elsewhere. We can brag about that, but when we spout that "we feed the world" with the bravado of a WWF wrestler, we've really gone too far.

We also like to point to the rising population—expected to be between 9.7 and 9.8 billion people between 2050 and 2080—as a way of waving off the criticisms of intensive agricultural production. Who among us has not quoted this explosive population prediction and its accompanying call for a 60 to 70 percent increase in food production? The problem for us is that some researchers are now growing more vocal in doubting whether these numbers will materialize. Several factors, including economic growth, rising education levels, and technological advancement, may press human fertility rates downward. International Institute for Applied Systems Analysis demographer Wolfgang Lutz (who has two Doctorates of Philosophy involving demographics and statistics) has projected that world population will more likely peak at about 8.9 billion by 2060 and decline to 7.8 billion by 2100.[307]

307. Wolfgang Lutz et al., eds., "Demographic and Human Capital Scenarios for the 21st Century: 2018 Assessment for 201 Countries," European Commission Joint Research Centre, 2018, p. 8.

Darrell Bricker and John Ibbitson, in their book *Empty Planet: The Shock of Global Population Decline*, argue that global population is headed for a steep decline, and that the decline has already begun in many places. Jorgen Randers, author of *The Limits to Growth*, predicts world population will peak at eight billion people in 2040. Swedish statistician Hans Rosling, founder of the Gapminder Institute, has dubbed 2000 as the year of "peak child." Deutsche Bank predicts an 8.7 billion person peak in 2055, with a decline to 8 billion before we welcome in 2101. Jack Bobo, the former State Department official now turned reasonable voice on agriculture and food (and one I admire) does not appear to take issue with the current UN population projections that we quote from memory. But he is quick to mention that the rise is not infinite, and that there is wide consensus that world population will retreat after its date with a peak in the 2050s.

Domestically, the United States is not contributing to population growth much either. "We are having fewer babies than ever," says Michael Brendan Dougherty, writing in *National Review*. "The fertility rate fell 4 percent in 2020, to its lowest ever. An America that currently has more than 330 million people in it produced in 2020 roughly the same number of babies as it did in 1979, when the total population was 225 million."[308] So much for English economist and demographer Thomas Malthus' theory that population growth will always tend to outrun the growth in food supply.

On this "population growth drives our industry" point, my cringing is the result of two simple beliefs. First, if these numbers are incorrect, then we ought not spout them like a church creed. In short, if they are wrong, we should stop saying them. Second, the coming population boom (or whisper) should not be used as a shield to defend any part of our work that needs to be improved. In my

308. Michael Dougherty, *Where the Heart Is*, National Review, pp. 18-19, November 15, 2021, also available at: *https://www.nationalreview.com/magazine/2021/11/15/where-the-heart-is/*.

view, the stronger argument is that our systems are sustainable, our farmers will continue to act responsibly, and the authors of the next generation of farming technology will continue to search for newer solutions and refine old ones. Any suggestion that we are excusing less than admirable behavior by saying "the population made me do it" eats away at our credibility and our commitment to sustainability.

There are other statistics that make me chuckle. We wring our hands over the increasing average age of our farmers, and I recognize that we worry about who will drive the tractors in another generation or two. But there is a silver lining there, too—the lengthening lifespan that we should all be applauding. We lament the "rising" imports of food, although in a few cases it is these imports that allowed us to create sustainable, year-round demand for crops we can grow only seasonally here in the U.S. Concomitantly, we sometimes suggest that the equilibrium between export market growth and domestic production growth will one day no longer exist, and that we will eventually see sustained price increases because of massive increases in export market demand. My money is on the economists who say it ain't so.

Enough of my meddling. My point here is merely to posit that our talking points will be tested more stringently over the next few decades than they ever have been before. Perhaps that should be the topic of another book. Our best defense in these tests is to guard our honesty and integrity. Under cross-examination, the worst thing we could do would be to not tell the truth.

RISK MANAGEMENT AND STRATEGERY

Third, we have to put our money—and our collective leadership—where our risks are.

In Washington and elsewhere, it seems there is an organization for everything. There's a Balloon Council and an organization of reptile keepers. There's even a sports organization for the armchair quarterbacks: The Sports Fan Coalition, which represents those of us who lose time and money on sports instead of profiting from them. In agriculture, the same is true. See the American Dehydrated Onion and Garlic Association, and the Dried Plum Association, both gifts of the diversity and ingenuity of the extraordinary story of California agriculture. Think about the lifecycle of a food ingredient, and there's an association or organization dedicated to policing the policy environment that impacts it. We have associations for seed, fertilizer, equipment manufacturers, equipment dealers, equipment financiers, creditors more generally, the commodities themselves (one for each commodity, of course), those focused on procuring workers, the land grant institutions, feed, oil from seed, protein producers and processors, ag truckers, retailers, rural energy providers, extension agents, and even the ag economists and educators. Not to mention the bureaus, cooperatives, broadcasters, departments of agriculture, conservationists, and organic folk. In no way am I attempting an exhaustive list. I'm smarter than that. And I preemptively apologize if I did not mention you. I meant to.

While this broad list of organizations and ag policy players may come in handy when planning a presidential ball or organizing a farm event at one of the national party conventions (with gratitude to those who manage such thankless tasks), it also presents liabilities for the future of agriculture. When speaking to a group of agriculture organization leaders a few years ago, I was afraid I would offend them when I said, based on my own personal observations, "We don't actually work together that much—we mainly work side by side very amicably." Instead, I saw dozens of heads in the room nod in agreement. We know it. We love each other. Mostly. And we love ag research, ag communication, and ag education. But when that door closes and vertical ag interests are alone with the decision-makers, it is all about Title I and Title II of the Farm Bill and whether I can juice the payment for my members, or get an earmark elsewhere for my association's individual interests.

There may be a notion that this adversarial process is as it should be, and that the elected officials are the ones that are supposed to sort out what is best for American agriculture in the long run. But do they?

When I arrived in Washington in 2015, I believed the era of regionalism in agriculture policy making was over. "We are all in this together," I thought. "There aren't many of us. We better stick together."

Boy was I wrong. As I mentioned in Chapter 7, we are all about tightening the government payment belt, as long as the belt is around some other aggie organization's waist, preferably one that doesn't operate in the committee chair's or ranking member's home state.

The risks this presents are twofold. First, at some level, our focus on issues that are parochial to our agricultural verticals frequently overshadow those risks that run horizontal across the entire ag industry. Our ag association structure has positioned us to work well on the emergency issue du jour, particularly acute ones facing our commodity-by-commodity organizations, but it has not equipped us to work across the entire industry on issues that creep along and grow in importance until they become existential threats (the undertows).

For example, while the legal risks I've mentioned in Chapter 8 seem to be more acute in animal agriculture and the crop-protection industry, the trial bar's tenacles are continuously feeling around for their next target. If you don't agree, watch daytime TV. Going forward, we must focus more on that non-urgent but important quadrant of risks that are eating away at the shoreline beneath our feet without us even knowing it. That is precisely what our critics are doing. Organizing, partnering, and leveraging one another in ways we do not seem immediately capable of replicating.

Some who read this will say "we do that." My response: Hahahahahahahahaha! Hahahahaha. Hahaha. Ha! I'm aware we have meetings and discuss doing it. We may even have names for cross-section collaboratives and coalitions. Working groups named after the resort where we first had aspirational dialogue. But do not forget, I sat with ag leaders on the other side of that door when it was closed. I was in the locker room at halftime. I have a very clear understanding of how public investment in research, social education about modern agriculture, and commitments to funding rural America end up as number seven, eight, and nine on the list of ten priorities. And how they stay there when the appropriations and authorizations are made.

The second risk presented by our vertical alignment is that the organizations I vaguely described above focus almost exclusively on the policy atmosphere in Washington. The whole point of this book is to make clear that the outsiders are moving the debates into other fora. In fact, they are moving them there precisely because they realize the other fora offer much less vigorously contested ground. And since Washington doesn't seem to be able to do much more than write letters to one another and delegate hard tasks to appointees (who they hope are either gone or reupped in four years), why would they waste much of their time inside I-495? The same is true to some extent for the ag verticals' focus on consumers and consumer trends. Food system critics appear to have observed that grass roots pushes against "big ag" and "big food"—consumer activism campaigns—weren't working. That explains why they have moved their focus to board rooms and the investor community.

Not a Mere High-Society Debate

Fourth, we have to understand that this debate is not merely about self-preservation. It is about our fellow, non-farming citizens and their freedom to live without worrying about food.

It was not that long ago that Norman Borlaug pioneered the Green Revolution, not because he was hoping to win the Nobel Peace Prize, which he ultimately did, but because the leading minds of his time had concluded that humanity's date with destiny was not going to end well. Unlike most of us, Borlaug had seen hunger up close and personal. In Mexico. In India. In his home state of Iowa. Many of the best and brightest around the world were ready to throw in the towel. In the late 1960s, Stanford Professor Paul Ehrlich famously wrote that "the battle to feed all of humanity is over." Professor Ehrlich predicted that millions—that is, hundreds of millions—of people around the world would starve to death because of lack of food in the 1970s. In his words, "At this late date nothing can prevent a substantial increase in the world death rate."

Some may point to the fact that world hunger still exists as proof that Ehrlich was correct. But that would overlook the fact that world hunger today is a fraction of what it was when he made his prediction. The prevalence of undernourishment in the world fell from 37 percent of the total population around 1970 to 14.8 percent in 2000, reaching a low of 10.6 percent in 2015.[309] All the while, we were almost systematically adding more people to the population total.

The precipitous decline of undernourishment happened precisely because of the Green Revolution. Agriculture is in the beginning phases of its fourth revolution, and the modern-day Paul Ehrlichs seem to be suggesting that the world should be thankful that they have showed up to fix us. Just in time. My concern is that they will

309. Ronald Bailey and Marian L. Tupy, "Ten Global Trends Every Smart Person Should Know," Cato Institute, 2020, pp. 127–28.

actually lead us into an era of less production, less efficiency, and less reliability. In short, a world with less food.

Moreover, those who point to continuing food insecurity in the developed world seem content to ignore that such insecurity is one of several manifestations of economic insecurity more generally, and not some proxy for the effectiveness of the agricultural community. It is not as if there are families who have upper-echelon housing, tip-top transportation, and clothing to match all the modern fashion trends but who do not have access to food. Like housing, transportation, and clothing, food security is almost always correlated with economic well-being. In the words of the Congressionally created bipartisan National Commission on Hunger, "America has no shortage of food, and no shortage of food assistance programs. . . . U.S. households experience hunger because of limited income due to a variety of factors, including low or underemployment, family instability, low educational attainment, exposure to violence, a history of racial or ethnic discrimination, personal choices, or a combination of these."[310] Notice there is no mention of a broken food system in the bipartisan commission's observations. A small victory, for sure.

Pointing to undernourishment in less developed society—in so-called third-world environments—as an agricultural problem ignores that hunger in those venues is frequently the byproduct of political instability: war, political violence, or corruption. It turns out that war zones are not the best place to turn around a six-row combine or debate the approvals for genetically engineered crops.

It has always perplexed me that it is the fault of our farmers that some people overeat while others are malnourished, but nobody blames the car manufacturers when they find themselves stuck behind a car going too slow or after being passed by one going too fast.

310. National Commission on Hunger, Final Report "*Freedom from Hunger: An Achievable Goal for the United States of America*," 2015 (pp. 1, 12) available at: *https://cybercemetery.unt.edu/archive/hungercommission/20151216222324/https://hungercommission.rti.org/Portals/0/SiteHtml/Activities/FinalReport/Hunger_Commission_Final_Report.pdf.*

If it is the farmers' and food system's fault that we eat the wrong things, why isn't it the vehicle makers' fault when someone drives too fast or too slow?

It is also perplexing to me that those who pair the Green Revolution of the middle of the last century with the purported agroecology catastrophe the farming community has foisted upon them today never articulate just what the alternative to Dr. Borlaug's increased efficiency should have been. I suppose we are left to fill in that all Borlaug did was delay the inevitable. Dr. Borlaug himself suggested that he has merely bought us time. Are they thinking that population decline would have been a better alternative than the productivity gains we've enjoyed because of fertilizer, pesticides, and scientific breakthroughs that have given us higher-yielding and lower input crops and animals? Unacceptable.

We cannot let our brethren forget that there was a time when our ancestors scavenged for chestnuts, and when they could no longer find them, they died. As late as the 1800s, bread was stretched with chalk or, in the worst circumstances, sawdust. In the words of historian Rachel Laudan, "No amount of nostalgia for the pastoral foods of the distant past can wish away the fact that our ancestors lived mean, short lives, constantly afflicted with diseases, many of which can be directly attributed to what they did and did not eat."[311]

Just what is at stake? Namely, that many of the authors of today's food movements have never stood at a meat or egg case and had to choose between $1.99 and $2.99.[312] That image—of a person hoping to stretch their food dollar while preparing something they can still enjoy—should haunt every person who wonders whether they should just yield the pen that will write the future of agriculture to the outsiders. The history of food is replete with cycles of boom and

311. Charles C. Ludington and Matthew Morse Booker, *Food Fights: How History Matters to Contemporary Food Debates*, University of North Carolina Press 2019, p. 270.

312. Admittedly, the origin of such a visual is up for debate, but I'm grateful that someone brought it to my attention.

bust, and with harrowing explanations of the hunger that ravaged many of our forebears.

In sum on this fourth point: I may never pour porridge or meal gruel into bowls in a third-world country, but I'll be darned if I'm going stand by and yield the floor to people who want to tape Humpty Dumpty together when he hasn't even fallen off the wall. Morally and ethically, there are just too many mouths to feed. There is only one right choice here. Our non-farming brethren are counting on us, whether they know it or not.

FARMER, OR COG IN A WHEEL?

Fifth, we have to explain that any "new" system of agriculture will involve tradeoffs. And most non-ag observers wouldn't like them. The aggies certainly won't.

The most ironic thing about all of the calls to reform, reshape, reroute, and revolutionize the farming and food system is that the people who are arguing most loudly for change can never seem to agree on precisely what the new system should look like. In fact, when I think about their buzzword solutions—like "new food systems"—I cannot seem to isolate precisely what the elements of such a new food system would be. The imagery is strong—shiny happy people holding hands—but beyond the approved vernacular (things like smallholder, regenerative, and free of factory farm gas), there is, as Secretary Perdue used to say, no "there" there. In fact, the suggestions that I have heard for "fixing" the food system would likely propagate more of the very things the critics seem to dislike about the current system.

The pressure to control, spread, and hedge costs is not going to go away in any system. Hampering the deployment of modern-day ag technology, including indoor agriculture for animals, would likely mean we end up with even larger scale operations—and environmental footprints—than we have today. We would need operations that can leverage greater and greater resources to manage the operations' risks and the market's volatility. We could expect a decrease in the number of industry players who are entrepreneurial at an individual level, and an increase in outside ownership of agricultural enterprises. Think more hedge companies and fewer Farm Credits. In some ways, this is already happening. But it would accelerate. Prepare for more farmers that are salaried farm managers, and more owners who sit on boards and attend annual meetings at nice hotels.

As this transformation took place, we could also expect that many of the privileges afforded to agricultural enterprises under federal and state laws would be more difficult to justify. It is one thing to keep the OSHA inspectors out of Uncle Ted's tin-covered barn, but Big Brother could become a fixture on farms that have to carefully monitor everything from the presence of methane to the pounds of nitrogen applied per acre. It is one thing to track this data because the market wants it and will pay for it. It's entirely different if Uncle Sam just says "give it to me."

Similarly, if the iconic view of the American farmer is trashed because policy makers are convinced that the system is broken from farm gate to dinner plate, those same policy makers will have little trouble concluding that greater regulation and oversight from government not only doesn't overly burden our farmers but is also required to make them act right.

Farm owners' autonomy is also at risk. One of the most heralded parts of farming is that so many people can do it in so many ways. If outsiders are successful in positioning themselves as the arbiters of what can and cannot happen down on the farm, their prescriptions will undoubtedly stifle the very individualism that drives some farmers to prefer green over red, or for my family to maintain our faith in blue.[313] When asked what kind of farmers we need, my answer has always been "yes!" Big, small, medium, conventional, organic, indoor, outside, urban, corn and grass feeding, antibiotic using and antibiotic free, users of old pick-up trucks or users addicted to the smell of new ones. If you don't believe greater oversight will ultimately lead to less choice, take a look at other highly regulated industries or try to close a real estate loan in less than thirty days.

Another staple of the "solutions" proffered by so many of agriculture's critics is to reduce the choices that can be made by farmers and food manufacturers (and, by extension, consumers). To lessen the number of options we have for farming and eating. To give the "good" farmers a stamp of approval and to frown at the conventional ones. To take away the "bad" food and limit the offerings to only the "good" food. Michael Pollan's second book was actually entitled *Food Rules*. In what world is this acceptable? Perhaps for the Europeans. But I do not believe this can be squared with the view that there is such a thing as American exceptionalism, where we are left to make for ourselves many of the decisions that drive our day, even if our decisions sometimes flirt with self-inflicted wounds. The "free people's suicide," as Os Guinness would say.

There is one more thing we stand to lose if outsiders write the ending: our leadership role. The innovation in our ag sector is the envy of the world. Such innovation is not inevitable, and it is certainly not automatic. The mantle of leadership carried by American farmers and food system leaders is a byproduct of their wit, wisdom, and commitment, but it also rests on functioning capital markets, a solid educational system, a reliable and predictable legal system, an informed media, and a rules-based international order. While we sometimes question whether these things do all still exist in the United States, we should admit they come closer to existing here

313. I'm referring here to farmers' loyalty to the color of their tractors. My advice to politicians is that tractor brand loyalty is about as strong as regional loyalty to barbecue. They would be wise to avoid insulting the choices in either category.

than they do anywhere else. What other place could come anywhere close to putting all of these winds at the backs of their farmers? Even if the pace of innovation could be matched somewhere else, would it continue to be deployed as impressively as it has been in the United States since the 1940s? Probably not.

To summarize, the wide array of agricultural leadership across the United States must better align itself to contest those creative forces that are shaping the future of farming and food. More attention must be paid to the question of how we can better align our mitigation efforts to ensure they address the industry's biggest threats. And there are some real threats—not all of them are mere misunderstandings. I've spoken mainly here about shifting our mindsets to focus on some of these outside risks. I've also proposed a bit of an architectural and structural revival of our farming, agribusiness, and food system leadership—a more horizontal engagement with less vertical focus. Implicit in this discussion is the commitment of resources required to tackle these threats. After admitting they exist and committing to confront and compete with them with honesty and integrity, we must pool our resources to better assess the critics' efforts and engage on forbearing them. No one group can do this alone. We have to organize the organizations. And make new friends. Like the outsiders are doing.

WINNING . . . AND HISTORY

Before coming to write the last few pages of this book, I read a lot of material. I talked to a lot of people. And I listened to a ton of presentations. Not to mention relying on a lifetime of experiences. Of all the ammunition I've read to support the view that it is our farmers and the key players in the greater agri-food value chain who have the better arguments, I never expected that it would be historians who would make me feel the most confident about that conclusion.

In the introduction to their book *Food Fights*, Charles Ludington and Matthew Booker gave me another example of the insider-outsider farming and food debate that I had not considered. They are historians, and as best I can tell they have spent most of their careers on college campuses. Perhaps that explains how they came to make the following insightful observation:

> *[W]hile scholars in the natural sciences who work on food generally see themselves as practical problem solvers who have slowly but surely helped to increase crop yield, extend shelf life, and thus reduce starvation—and in wealthy countries to provide consumers with all sorts of specialty foods and drinks—scholars in the humanities and social sciences have overwhelmingly come to food studies from the perspective that the current American food system is unhealthy in almost every way.*

Ludington and Booker seem to be saying that even on the same college campus, there are extraordinarily bright people who hold diametrically opposing views of farming and food. And they seem to be struck by the same conundrum that I teed up in Chapter 2: if one says Humpty Dumpty has fallen and the other says he is still intact, they cannot both be correct.

So who is wrong and who is right? I have not hidden the ball that I believe the farmers and food system insiders are right. I also believe, as laid out earlier in this chapter, it is not just our pride that we are defending. The stakes are higher than that.

The irony for me is that I think we are, at the moment, still winning. Other industries (and political candidates) would love to have our polling numbers. Gallup consistently finds, in their image ratings of U.S. industries, that Americans like their farmers and agriculture.

In fact, in 2021, across twenty-five industry sectors, only four were rated positively. Three of those four are iterations of farming and food (farming and agriculture, the restaurant industry, and the grocery industry).[314] In private polling that I've had the opportunity to personally review, urbanites think as highly of farming and agriculture as rural folk do. We are a crowned industry, but rather than wearing that mantle proudly, we seem to like to play the role of the underdog, constantly lamenting that people just do not think highly enough of us. My worry is that we are going to wish that status into being.

Those who called for and predicted a foodie revolution have had to save face by recalibrating the timelines of their prognostications. Most Americans do not believe agriculture is killing us. Or the planet. At least not right now.

That said, shame on us if we are so naive as to think that all we need to do to win over our detractors and prevent their success is to tell our story. We have to avoid both complacency and combativeness, use collaboration where we can, and intense competition where we can't. That competition is going to occur in new venues. At a minimum, we should show up and avoid forfeiting.

In short, we are winning. At the moment. We just can't get tired of winning.

The plane is not going to wait.

---

314. Brenan, Megan and Jeffrey M. Jones, "Image Ratings of Several U.S. Industries Tumble," Gallup, September 13, 2021, available at: *https://news.gallup.com/poll/354653/image-ratings-several-industries-tumble.aspx*.

STAYING ENGAGED

Congratulations! You made it to the back of the book. It can be lonely back here, so thanks for coming. Hopefully you're left with a sense that this message, and the efforts to address the *Farmers versus Foodies* challenge, need our attention and our action. There are at least two ways through which you can help further the message and the solutions outlined here.

HAVE RAY ATTEND YOUR NEXT MEETING

If you appreciate what you've read here, consider working with Ray to have him speak at your next meeting. He has spoken in more than forty states, to groups as small as a dozen and to audiences in the thousands. Clients include the National Pork Board, National FFA Organization, Farm Equipment Manufacturers Association, EDGE Dairy Cooperative, numerous farm credits and farm bureaus, and dozens of others. He manages his speaking availability through his personal company Short Rows Leadership, LLC, which you can learn more about at: shortrowsleadership.com.

BUY BOOKS IN BULK

Have a reading group or just want to share the book with a few friends? Contact Ray for bulk purchase discounts starting with as few as ten books. E-mail him directly for more information at:

ray@shortrowsleadership.com.

A FAVOR

If you enjoyed the book, please consider leaving a review on Amazon!

About the Author

Ray A. Starling is an attorney, speaker, law professor, and public policy professional who has focused most of his career on agriculture law and policy. After growing up on a diversified Century Farm in southeast North Carolina, he studied agricultural education at NC State University and then attended the University of North Carolina School of Law, graduating with honors. He has counseled State Supreme Court Justices, a Commissioner of Agriculture, a North Carolina Speaker of the House and U.S. Senator who sat on the Senate Agriculture Committee, and the U.S. Secretary of Agriculture. He also staffed the National Economic Council at the White House, serving as the Special Assistant to the President for Agriculture, Agriculture Trade, and Food Assistance. He now serves as the General Counsel of the NC Chamber and the President of the NC Chamber's Legal Institute in Raleigh.